Volume 13: How to Use Sequential Statistical Methods

The ASQC Basic References in Quality Control: Statistical Techniques

John A. Cornell, PhD, and Samuel S. Shapiro, PhD, Editors

Volume 13: How to Use Sequential Statistical Methods

by

Thomas P. McWilliams

American Society for Quality Control
310 West Wisconsin Avenue
Milwaukee, Wisconsin 53203

Volume 13: How to Use Sequential Statistical Methods

by

Thomas P. McWilliams

ISBN 0-87389-049-3

Printed in the United States of America

The ASQC Basic References in Quality Control: Statistical Techniques is a continuing literature project of ASQC's Statistics Division. Its aim is to present the latest statistical techniques in a form which is easily followed by the quality control practitioner so that these procedures can be readily applied to solve industrial quality problems.

Suggestions as to subject matters to be covered and format of the booklets are welcome and will be considered for future editions. Such suggestions should be sent to one of the co-editors.

Volumes Published

How to Analyze Data with Simple Plots (W. Nelson)
How to Perform Continuous Sampling (CSP) (K. Stephens)
How to Test Normality and Other Distributional Assumptions (S. Shapiro)
How to Perform Skip-Lot and Chain Sampling (K. Stephens)
How to Run Mixture Experiments for Product Quality (J. Cornell)
How to Analyze Reliability Data (W. Nelson)
How and When to Perform Bayesian Acceptance Sampling (T. W. Calvin)
How to Apply Response Surface Methodology (J. Cornell)
How to Use Regression Analysis in Quality Control (D. C. Crocker)
How to Plan an Accelerated Life Test — Some Practical Guidelines
   (W. Meeker and G. Hahn)
How to Perform Statistical Tolerance Analysis (N. D. Cox)
How to Choose the Proper Sample Size (G. G. Brush)

In order to purchase volumes write to: American Society for Quality Control, 310 West Wisconsin Avenue, Milwaukee, Wisconsin 53203, USA.

Foreword

The ASQC Basic References in Quality Control: Statistical Techniques is a literature project of the Statistics Division of the ASQC. The series' review board consists of Saul Blumenthal, Joseph W. Foster, Alan J. Gross, Gerald J. Hahn, Norman L. Johnson, H. Alan Lasater, Edward A. Sylvestre, and Harrison M. Wadsworth, Jr., supplemented (for the current volume, 13th in the series) by Leo Aroian.

In the Statistics Division Newsletter, Volume 1, Number 1 (February 21, 1980), Philip B. Crosby (then president of the ASQC) called the comprehension and handling of statistics "...the most basic of needs for all of us..." He went on to state that "without numerical information in its most precise form, we cannot complete our responsibility to management and other fellow employees. And without the tools to first comprehend and then explain the analysis, we are equally impotent."

This booklet is a primer in the construction of sequential sampling plans. The material presented enables the reader to easily construct such plans to satisfy specified AQL and RQL requirements for binomial, hypergeometric, Poisson, normal, and exponential situations. The booklet demonstrates the savings available from the use of sequential procedures. It contains formulas for both the design of the plan and the construction of OC and ASN curves. A computer program is included for obtaining precise values for these two evaluation curves. Rules are suggested for the inclusion of truncation points and the effect of the truncation on the OC and ASN curves is discussed. A sequential procedure for the comparison of two binomial parameters, which is useful in clinical trials, is described. The ideas presented are all illustrated with simple examples. There are many references to more advanced concepts.

The author of this booklet is Thomas P. McWilliams, PhD. Dr. McWilliams is an assistant professor with the Management Science Group, College of Business Administration, Northeastern University in Boston. He has a clear and concise style of writing and has drawn on his nine years of experience in teaching and statistical consulting to prepare an understandable guide on how to use sequential statistical techniques.

Samuel S. Shapiro
Florida International University
Miami, Florida
September 1987

Table of Contents

Abstract

This volume presents a basic description of how to use *sequential statistical models*. The reader is led through the text by examples that illustrate the technique being discussed. The text begins with a basic explanation of sequential procedures. It then applies these fundamentals to developing formulas for use with binomial sampling plans and goes on to cover sampling plans for hypergeometric and Poisson distributions. One subsection is devoted to comparative binomial trials. The following section applies these ideas to variables sampling and covers tests for the mean where the standard deviation is known or unknown, and a test for variability. The next section describes a test for the exponential distribution. The booklet concludes with discussions on how to calculate the OC and ASN functions directly and how to obtain parameter estimates when sequential procedures are used. A computer program is included that can be used to compute the OC and ASN functions for the binomial sampling model.

1. Introduction

The practice of making a decision or statement regarding a *population* of measurements based only on *sample* information is frequently encountered in the practice of statistical quality control. For example, hypothesis testing procedures are used in lot acceptance decisions, in maintaining current control of the output of a process, etc. In most applications the hypothesis test is designed (a sample size n is chosen, along with "accept" and "reject" regions for the test statistic) to meet specified probabilities of Type I and Type II errors and to have an acceptable operating characteristic (OC) function. A total of n observations is made, and the final decision is then based on the calculated value of some test statistic. This procedure is known as a fixed sample size hypothesis test, as the sample size n is determined in advance of the sampling process.

Sequential hypothesis testing procedures take a different approach. In general, a sequential procedure can be defined as any test procedure where the sample size required to make the decision is *not* known in advance but rather is determined by the sample results. Sequential procedures take the approach that a decision to accept or reject the null hypothesis (H_0) should be made *as soon as* convincing evidence is available either in support of or against H_0. Sample information is processed and evaluated as it becomes available, rather than at the end of the entire sampling process. Time and money are *not* wasted by taking more measurements than are needed to make the accept or reject decision confidently. For a wide variety of hypothesis testing situations encountered in the practice of statistical quality control, substantial benefits can be attained by replacing traditional fixed sample size procedures with sequential procedures.

This text focuses on sequential methods of interest to the quality practitioner, with particular emphasis on hypothesis testing. Examples of sequential test plans and the underlying logic behind sequential testing can be found in Sections 2 and 3. Section 4 contains detailed examples illustrating the design and evaluation of sequential test plans. The direct method of evaluating sequential plan properties is presented in Section 5, while sequential estimation is discussed briefly in section 6.

2. Sequential Test Plans

Sequential test plans gather sample information only until enough is available to make a decision confidently. The number of observations that the plan requires is *not* known in advance. This is the distinguishing feature of a sequential plan: The sample size is a random variable determined by the observed data, rather than a predetermined fixed value. Throughout this text we will use N to denote the random sample size, or *decisive sample number* (DSN) of a sequential process. Several sequential plans, of increasing complexity, are illustrated in this section. These plans are all viable alternatives to the fixed sample size plan of the following example.

Example 2.1:

In a particular lot acceptance sampling procedure, incoming units arriving in large lots are classified as being either conforming or nonconforming. Let p represent the true proportion of nonconforming units in the lot. Lots are acceptable if p = 0.01 (AQL value) or less, otherwise they are unacceptable. Consider testing

$$H_0: p \le .01 \text{ versus } H_1: p > .01.$$

One possible fixed sample size test plan (MIL-STD-105D Plan J, Single Sampling, Normal Inspection) is to take n = 80 observations and reject the lot if X, the number of observed nonconforming units, is 3 or more. Otherwise, the lot is accepted. This plan has a Type I error probability of $\alpha = 0.047$ and a Type II error probability at, for example, an RQL value of p = 0.06 of $\beta = 0.134$. The OC function for the plan is shown in Figure 1, along with OC functions for test plans which will be discussed in Sections 2.2 and 2.3.

Figure 1: OC Functions for Binomial Sampling

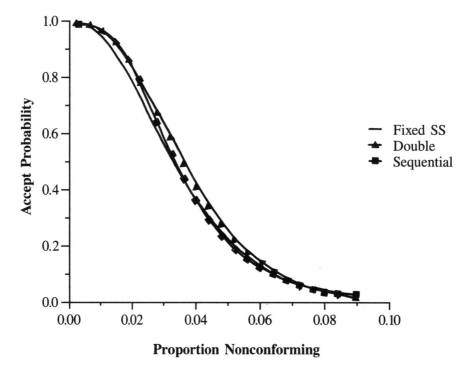

2.1 Curtailed Test Plan

The first example of a sequential plan is a *curtailed* test plan. Curtailed test plans are based on fixed sample size test plans, with the modification that the sampling process stops as soon as the decision is certain.

Example 2.2:

For the plan of Example 2.1, if on the 30th observation the 3rd noncomforming unit is observed, then the decision (reject the lot) is determined and there would be no need to observe 50 more items. If by observation number 79 only one nonconforming unit had been observed, then the decision (accept the lot) would be determined since the maximum number of nonconforming units attainable in the sample of size 80 would be two, which is below the test's rejection value. These examples illustrate the logic of test curtailment. In general, a fixed sample size plan having sample size n and reject value R can be curtailed by:

- rejecting H_0 as soon as R nonconforming units are observed; and

- accepting H_0 on observation number k if the number of nonconforming units X_k observed at that point is strictly less than $(R + k - n)$.

The OC function for the curtailed test will be identical to that of the corresponding fixed sample size test.

The curtailed plan is appealing because, in most cases, the decisive sample number N will be strictly less than the fixed sample size value of n = 80. (Obviously N cannot exceed n.) One way to evaluate the performance of the curtailed test procedure is to calculate the expected value of N, called the *average sample number* (ASN). This value is a function of p, the true proportion of nonconforming units in the lot: If p is large we can expect to quickly observe three nonconforming units and terminate the test procedure; if p is small termination is unlikely to happen quickly, and all 80 or nearly 80 observations may be required. Therefore, rather than specifying a single value, an *ASN function* is calculated. While the usefulness of a fixed sample size procedure can be determined by examining its OC function, sequential procedures should be evaluated based on both the OC and ASN functions.

Figure 2: ASN Functions for Binomial Sampling

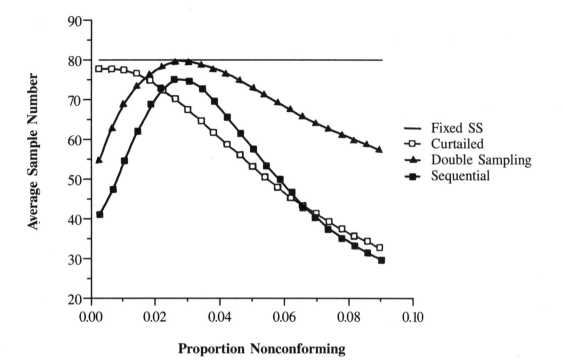

The ASN function for the curtailed plan of Example 2.2 is shown in Figure 2. The main benefit of using the curtailed plan is readily apparent: On the average, fewer obervations will be required to make the decision. Although the savings in required observations is not substantial for acceptable lots (small p-values), the savings can be significant for unacceptable lots. At p = 0.06 (the RQL value), the decision requires an average of 46.9 observations, a savings of 41 percent over the fixed sample size plan. At p = 0.09, the ASN is 33.0, a 59 percent savings. It is important to recognize that the two plans have identical OC curves, so this savings is realized at no loss of ability in correctly distinguishing between H_0 and H_1.

2.2 Double Sampling Plan

The curtailed test plan is a very basic type of sequential plan. A more sophisticated sequential test plan is a *double sampling* plan. In double sampling a fixed number of units n_1 are tested and the number of nonconforming units X_1 observed. Depending on the value of X_1, the decision is made to either accept the lot, reject the lot, or acquire additional observations (continue to sample). If the decision is to continue, then an additional n_2 units are tested and X_2 nonconforming units are observed. The final decision is then made based on $(X_1 + X_2)$, the cumulative number of nonconforming units observed. The flowchart in Figure 3 illustrates the logic of the plan.

Figure 3: Double Sampling Flowchart

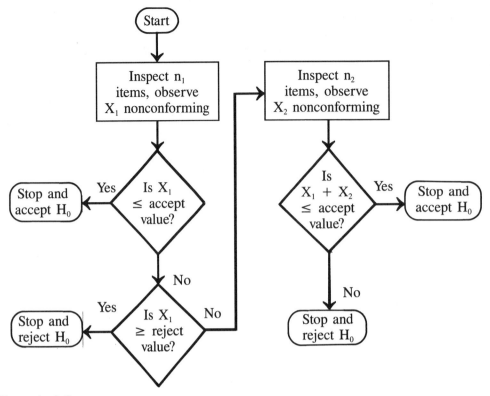

Example 2.3:

MIL-STD-105D (Plan J) gives a double sampling plan designed to match the OC function of the fixed sample size plan of Example 2.1. An initial sample of size $n_1 = 50$ is taken, and the lot is accepted if $X_1 = 0$ and rejected if $X_1 \geq 3$. Otherwise, a second sample of size $n_2 = 50$ is taken. The lot is then accepted if the cumulative value $(X_1 + X_2)$ is 3 or less, otherwise the lot is rejected. The OC and ASN functions for this plan are shown in Figures 1 and 2, respectively.

As with the curtailed plan, the double sampling plan yields a reduction in the expected number of observations required (ASN) to make a decision at all levels of p. In this case the reduction is most substantial at small p-values and at large p-values, as in these cases the decision is most likely to be made based only on the initial 50 observations. When $p = 0.01$, the ASN is equal to 69.1 and the second sample will be required 38 percent of the time. When $p = 0.09$, the ASN is 57.6 and the second sample will be required only 15 percent of the time. For "intermediate" values of p the second sample will often be required, increasing the ASN value. For example, when $p = 0.04$, the second sample will be required 55 percent of the time and the ASN is 77.3. In contrast to the curtailed plan, it is now possible to need *more* observations (100 versus 80) with a sequential procedure. A reduction in sample size will occur *on the average,* but cannot be guaranteed in any specific instance. The OC curves for the fixed and double sampling plans match quite well, so there is no loss in decision-making ability.

2.3 Wald's Sequential Plan

The most complex, but potentially most valuable, sequential test plans considered in this booklet are based on Wald's (1947) work in sequential analysis. The underlying logic is discussed in Section 3. For these plans, accept and reject values are calculated *for each step of the sampling process.*

If the cumulative number of nonconforming units X_i observed on the ith observation exceeds the ith observation's reject value, then the process stops and the lot is rejected. If X_i is less than the ith observation's accept value, the process stops and the lot is accepted. Otherwise, another unit is tested. This process continues until a decision is reached.

Figure 4: Sequential Test Plan, Binomial Sampling

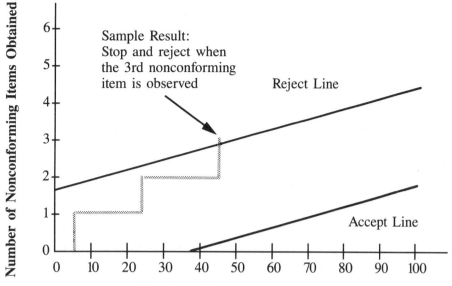

Table 1: Sequential Test Plan, Binomial Sampling

Observation Number	Accept Value	Observed Nonconforming	Reject Value	Observation Number	Accept Value	Observed Nonconforming	Reject Value
1	**	0	**	31	**	2	3
2	**	0	2	32	**	2	3
3	**	0	2	33	**	2	3
4	**	0	2	34	**	2	3
5	**	0	2	35	**	2	3
6	**	0	2	36	**	2	3
7	**	0	2	37	**	2	3
8	**	0	2	38	0	2	3
9	**	0	2	39	0	2	3
10	**	1	2	40	0	2	3
11	**	1	2	41	0	2	3
12	**	1	2	42	0	2	3
13	**	1	2	43	0	3	3
14	**	1	2	44	0	**REJECT!**	3
15	**	1	3	45	0		3
16	**	1	3	46	0		3
17	**	1	3	47	0		3
18	**	1	3	48	0		3
19	**	1	3	49	0		3
20	**	1	3	50	0		3
21	**	1	3	51	0		4
22	**	1	3	52	0		4
23	**	2	3	53	0		4
24	**	2	3	54	0		4
25	**	2	3	55	0		4
26	**	2	3	56	0		4
27	**	2	3	57	0		4
28	**	2	3	58	0		4
29	**	2	3	59	0		4
30	**	2	3	60	0		4

Example 2.4:

A Wald sequential plan designed to match the OC curves of Examples 2.1 through 2.3 is illustrated graphically in Figure 4 and tabulated in Table 1. The calculations required to generate this plan can be found in Section 4.1.1. Either the graphical or the table format could be used to apply the plan. Using the table, the inspector fills in and continuously checks the cumulative number of nonconforming units observed against the values of Table 1. With the graph, the number of units inspected versus nonconforming units observed is plotted and the result compared to the accept and reject boundary lines. In either case, the process stops as soon as an accept or reject boundary is crossed. The OC and ASN functions for this plan are shown in Figures 1 and 2, respectively.

The Wald plan's ASN function is similar in shape to that of the double sampling plan, but the savings achieved in the average number of required observations is generally greater and sometimes substantially greater. The OC function matches the others quite well, so once again this savings is achieved at no loss in the ability of the test procedure to correctly choose between H_0 and H_1.

2.4 Truncated Sequential Plan

Like the double sampling plan, there is a possibility with the Wald sequential plan that the decisive sample number N will exceed the fixed sample size plan value of 80. In fact, *conceptually,* a Wald sequential test could require any number of observations! This problem is occasionally cited as a reason not to use Wald's procedure. The problem can be solved by specifying a maximum tolerable number of observations, which we will denote m_0. Wald's boundaries are used until the decision is made or until m_0 observations have been made. If a decision has not been reached, based on Wald's boundaries, by the m_0th observation, then the process stops and the decision is made based on predetermined accept and reject criteria. This plan is known as a *truncated sequential test plan.*

Example 2.5:

Consider the plan presented in Example 2.4, but suppose that the sampling process will be terminated if a decision has not been reached as of observation number $m_0 = 165$ (guidance in determining the value of m_0 is presented in Section 4.1.1). At the 165th observation, the lot will be rejected or accepted according to which sequential test boundary line the observed number of nonconforming items comes closest. This plan is presented in Figure 5 (the horizontal portion of the reject boundary line indicates curtailment when the truncation point's rejection value is reached). The OC and ASN functions are compared to the corresponding functions for the nontruncated sequential plan in Figures 6A and 6B.

Figure 5: Truncated Sequential Test Plan, Binomial Sampling

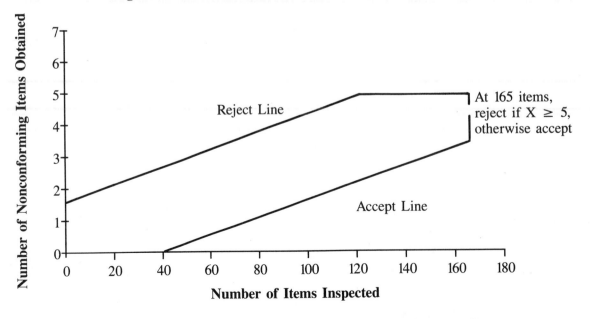

6

In this case the incorporation of a truncation point into the test plan has no practical impact on the OC function, which is not surprising since truncation will rarely occur. For example, in the high ASN case of $p = 0.04$, truncation will occur only 6 percent of the time. At this value of p, truncation reduces the ASN from 67.8 to 64.4, a reduction of 5 percent. The standard deviation of the ASN is reduced by a more substantial 19 percent, so the degree of uncertainty regarding the value of N is reduced. The probability of rejecting H_0 at $p = 0.04$ is 0.629 for the usual sequential plan versus 0.631 for the truncated plan. Truncating the plan in this manner provides assurance that an unreasonably large sample size can never occur, reduces the average sample number for *all* values of p, and does not adversely affect the OC function. Truncation procedures are discussed further in Section 4.

3. Wald Sequential Test Procedure

The sequential test plans described in Examples 2.4 and 2.5 are based on a procedure first developed by Wald (1947). This procedure uses the *likelihood ratio* to determine, after each observation is made, whether enough information is available to accept or reject the null hypothesis. Let $f_1(\underline{x},k)$ represent the likelihood function of the sample result $\underline{x} = (X_1,....,X_k)$ when H_1 is true, and let $f_0(\underline{x},k)$ represent the likelihood function when H_0 is true. The ratio $R_k = f_1(\underline{x},k)/f_0(\underline{x},k)$ is the likelihood ratio. When this ratio is large, evidence points to f_1 as the true likelihood function, and thus to H_1. When small, evidence points to H_0. Intermediate values are inconclusive, leading to the decision to continue sampling. A sequential test can be performed by calculating R_k after each new observation is available, and:

(i) stopping with a "Reject H_0" decision if $R_k > A$;
(ii) stopping with an "Accept H_0" decision if $R_k < B$; and
(iii) continuing to sample if $B \leq R_k \leq A$.

Boundary values A and B are chosen to satisfy Type I and Type II error specifications for the hypothesis test. Letting α and β represent the probabilities of these errors, respectively, A and B are calculated according to

$$A = (1 - \beta)/\alpha \qquad\qquad B = \beta/(1 - \alpha).$$

A sequential test based on these boundaries will have error probabilities *approximately* equal to the nominal α and β values. The calculation of actual error probabilities α' and β' is complex and will be discussed in Section 5. Wald showed that the actual error probabilities cannot be substantially larger than the nominal values, deriving the inequalities

$$\alpha' \leq \alpha/(1 - \beta)$$
$$\beta' \leq \beta/(1 - \alpha)$$
$$\alpha' + \beta' \leq \alpha + \beta.$$

Since α and β are typically small values in practice, the upper bounds for α' and β' will be quite close to α and β. In addition, the third inequality insures that α' and β' cannot both be larger than the corresponding nominal values, so the worst case would be for one actual error probability to be slightly larger than its nominal value.

Hypothesis tests based on the likelihood ratio can be expressed in a simple form for many cases of interest to the quality practitioner. These cases and other applications of sequential methods are presented in the following section.

4. Applications of Sequential Methods

4.1 Attributes Sampling

4.1.1 Binomial Distribution

Consider testing H_0: $p = p_0$ versus H_1: $p = p_1$, where $p_1 > p_0$. This corresponds to the lot acceptance sampling example used throughout Section 2. If the lot size is large relative to the anticipated sample size, the binomial model is appropriate. Let $X_i = 0$ if the ith observation results in a conforming item, $X_i = 1$ if nonconforming. Let

$$d_k = \sum_{i=1}^{k} X_i, \tag{4-1}$$

the number of nonconforming items found in the first k observations. The likelihood functions under H_0 and H_1 are given by

$$f_0(\underline{x},k) = (p_0)^{d_k}(1-p_0)^{k-d_k} \tag{4-2}$$
$$f_1(\underline{x},k) = (p_1)^{d_k}(1-p_1)^{k-d_k}.$$

The likelihood ratio is equal to

$$R_k = (p_1/p_0)^{d_k}[(1-p_1)/(1-p_0)]^{k-d_k}. \tag{4-3}$$

The calculation of R_k at each stage of the sampling process is tedious, but it can be shown mathematically that comparing R_k to A and B at each stage is equivalent to the following procedure:

(i) stop and reject H_0 if $d_k > h_2 + sk$;
(ii) stop and accept H_0 if $d_k < -h_1 + sk$; and
(iii) continue to sample if $-h_1 + sk \leq d_k \leq h_2 + sk$

where

$$r_1 = \ln(p_1/p_0) \qquad\qquad r_2 = \ln[(1-p_0)/(1-p_1)] \tag{4-4}$$
$$a = \ln A = \ln\{(1 - \beta)/\alpha\} \qquad b = -\ln B = \ln[(1 - \alpha)/\beta]$$
$$s = r_2/(r_1 + r_2) \qquad\qquad h_1 = b/(r_1 + r_2)$$
$$h_2 = a/(r_1 + r_2).$$

In a plot of d_k versus k, the equations $d_k = -h_1 + sk$ and $d_k = h_2 + sk$ represent parallel lines, namely the "accept" and "reject" boundary lines. The test can be carried out by simply plotting d_k versus k at each stage of the process and continuing to sample until either the accept or reject boundary is crossed.

Example 4.1:

A fixed sample size test procedure for testing H_0: $p = 0.01$ versus H_1: $p = 0.06$ is given in Example 2.1 (MIL-STD-105D Plan J; n = 80, reject number =3). This plan results in error probabilities $\alpha = 0.047$ and $\beta = 0.134$. To find a sequential procedure with approximately the same α and β values, calculate

$$r_1 = \ln(0.06/0.01) = 1.792$$
$$r_2 = \ln[(1 - 0.01)/(1 - 0.06)] = 0.0518$$
$$A = (1 - \beta)/\alpha = (1 - 0.134)/0.047 = 18.426$$
$$B = \beta/(1 - \alpha) = 0.134/(1 - 0.047) = 0.1406$$
$$a = \ln(18.426) = 2.914$$
$$b = -\ln(0.1406) = 1.962$$
$$s = 0.0518/(1.792 + 0.0518) = 0.028$$
$$h_1 = 1.962/(1.792 + 0.0518) = 1.06$$
$$h_2 = 2.914/(1.792 + 0.0518) = 1.58$$

so the boundaries of the sequential test are determined, respectively, by the equations

$$d_k = 1.58 + 0.028k$$
$$d_k = -1.06 + 0.028k.$$

These boundaries are shown in Figure 4. Alternately, accept and reject values can be calculated for each value of k (rounding up for the reject value, down for the accept value) and presented in the form of Table 1. In either case, an inspector can quickly check after each observation is made to see whether the test terminates and, if so, what decision is reached.

OC and ASN Function Calculations

The calculation of exact OC or ASN function values for the sequential test of Example 4.1 can be tedious. For a very rough idea of the shape of these functions, five points may be easily *approximated*. Let $P_A(p)$ represent the probability of accepting H_0 and let ASN(p) represent the average sample number, both expressed as a function of the true proportion of nonconforming items p. Calculate the following

$\underline{p}$	$\underline{P_A(p)}$	$\underline{ASN(p)}$	
0.0	1.0	$[[h_1/s]] + 1$	(4-5)
p_0	$\approx 1 - \alpha$	$\approx [(1 - \alpha) h_1 - \alpha h_2] / [s - p_0]$	
s	$\approx h_2/(h_1 + h_2)$	$\approx h_1 h_2/ [s(1 - s)]$	
p_1	$\approx \beta$	$\approx [(1 - \beta) h_2 - \beta h_1] / [p_1 - s]$	
1.0	0.0	$[[h_2 / (1 - s)]] + 1.$	

The symbol $[[\cdot]]$ represents the greatest integer function. Rough sketches of either the OC or ASN function can be obtained by connecting these five points. The formulas given previously at p_0, s, and p_1 are specific cases of more general formulas, which can be used to approximate the entire OC and ASN functions. The more general formulas and examples of their use can be found in Appendix A. Numerical results given in the Appendix show that the approximation formulas should be used with caution as they may not be particularly accurate. Garrison and Hickey (1984) give a BASIC program to calculate accept and reject boundaries and OC and ASN values using these approximation formulas.

It is also possible to obtain exact (to the limits of computer accuracy) OC and ASN values using the *direct method* developed by Aroian (1968, 1976). This method is discussed in detail in Section 5, and Appendix B contains a FORTRAN program for calculating OC and ASN functions for one-sided sequential test plans based on binomial sampling. Table 2 illustrates typical program output. This program was used to generate the curves shown in Figures 1 and 2. Calculated error probabilities for the sequential test are $\alpha = 0.027$ and $\beta = 0.135$. The goal of matching the fixed sample size test values of 0.047 and 0.134 has effectively been satisfied (the sequential test is actually more conservative at p_0). The exact ASN value, at $p = p_0 = 0.01$, is equal to 54.9 with a standard deviation of 32.8. The probability of exceeding the fixed sample size test value of n = 80 is calculated to be equal to 0.11. If p *is* equal to 0.01, the use of the sequential rather than the fixed sample procedure will save, on the average, about 25 observations. However, the sequential plan will require *more* than 80 observations about 11 percent of the time, so this savings is not guaranteed in any particular instance. At $p = p_1 = 0.06$, the exact ASN is 48.0 with a standard deviation of 37.8. The probability of needing more than 80 observations to complete the test is equal to 0.15. The "worst case" occurs around p = 0.028, where the ASN equals 75.5 with a standard deviation of 60.5. At this p value, more than 80 observations would be required about 29 percent of the time. However, even in this case, an average savings of five observations is realized when compared to the fixed sample size test.

Table 2: Direct Method Results, Binomial Sampling

```
$ RUN SHORT

INPUT PLOW, PHIGH, AND PDEL
.01   .08   .01

IF YOU WISH P(N>M), INPUT M. ELSE INPUT ZERO.
79

INPUT COMMON SLOPE, ACCEPT INTERCEPT, REJECT INTERCEPT
.028  -1.06  1.58

INPUT TRUNCATION VALUE AND REJECT NUMBER
(-1 IF DECISION BASED ON CLOSEST BOUNDARY)
80   3
```

P	ACC. PR. (OC Values)	REJ. PR.	ASN	S.D.	P (N > 79)
0.01	0.9554	0.0446 (α)	48.86	17.54	.0913
0.02	0.8018	0.1982	53.26	20.01	.1672
0.03	0.6033	0.3967	52.68	21.23	.1707
0.04	0.4204	0.5796	49.31	22.09	.1367
0.05	0.2779	0.7221	44.79	22.36	.0954
0.06	0.1773 (β)	0.8227	40.06	22.00	.0608
0.07	0.1105	0.8895	35.61	21.15	.0363
0.08	0.0680	0.9320	31.64	20.01	.0206

Truncation

As discussed in Section 2.4, a disturbing feature of the sequential test is the possibility, however remote, that an unreasonably large number of observations will be needed to reach a decision. This can be avoided by *truncating* the test at some predetermined maximum acceptable number of observations m_0. This should be done with caution, as truncation can have an impact on the test's OC function.

A very conservative scheme is to use a large truncation value, which will result in no practical impact on the OC function while providing some level of protection against the need for an unreasonable number of observations. For example, Burr (1976) recommends truncating at $3 \cdot (\max\{ASN(p_0), ASN(p_1)\})$. The decision to accept or reject can then be made depending on which boundary d_k is closest to. In the example in this section this would mean truncating at $3 \cdot (\max \{54.9, 48.0\}) \approx 165$. Figures 6A and 6B illustrate the impact, on the OC and ASN Functions, of truncating the test at $m_0 = 165$. For example, the ASN at P_0 is reduced from 54.9 to 54.2. The reduction is trivial due to the fact that, with this large value, truncation will occur about 1 percent of the time so it has little impact on the results.

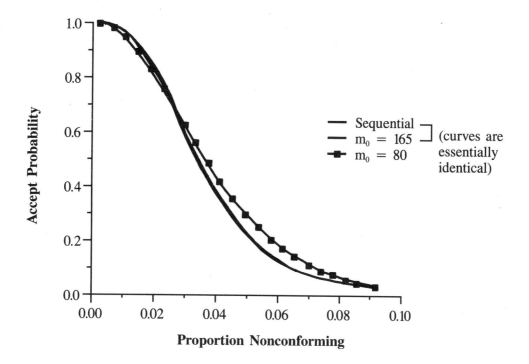

Figure 6A: Sequential Plan OC Functions, Binomial Sampling

(curves are essentially identical)

— Sequential
— $m_0 = 165$
■ $m_0 = 80$

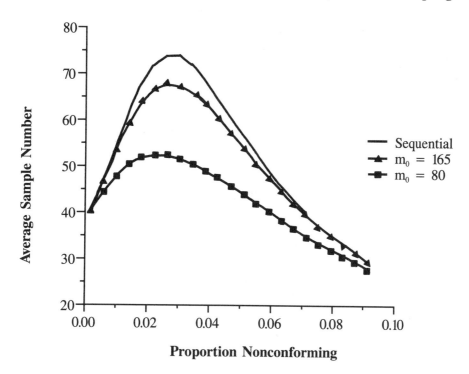

Figure 6B: Sequential Plan ASN Functions, Binomial Sampling

— Sequential
▲ $m_0 = 165$
■ $m_0 = 80$

Similarly, the ASN at p_1 is reduced from 48.0 to 47.0, and truncation will occur less than 0.5 percent of the time. A more substantial reduction occurs in the "worst case" situation of $p = 0.028$, when the ASN is reduced from 75.4 to 69.0, with a reduction in standard deviation from 60.5 to 42.8. Truncation will occur 4 percent of the time. In this case truncation saves six observations on the average, reduces the uncertainty regarding the number of observations required, and ensures that no more than 165 observations will be required.

Figure 5 illustrates the sequential test plan truncated at $m_0 = 165$. The closest boundary criteria leads to rejection if d_{165} is five or larger, acceptance otherwise. Since the observation of five nonconforming items prior to the truncation point will inevitably lead to rejection, the test is curtailed, as indicated by the horizontal portion of the reject boundary, at $d_k = 5$. The OC functions for the traditional and conservatively truncated ($m_0 = 165$) sequential test plans are compared in Figure 6A, and it is seen that they are functionally equivalent.

Figures 6A and 6B also illustrate the effect of truncation at a much smaller value, namely the fixed sample size test value of $n = m_0 = 80$. When considering smaller truncation values the OC function should be checked (using, for example, the direct method program) to ensure that the performance of the test procedure is not significantly impaired by the truncation process. Aroian (1976) recommends truncating at either $1.2n$, where n represents the sample size of an equivalent fixed sample size test, or at n itself. These more aggressive approaches to truncating should not be used without assurance that the sequential plan's OC function is not seriously degraded.

4.1.2 Hypergeometric Distribution

Consider the lot acceptance example of Section 4.1.1., but suppose that the anticipated sample size is "large" relative to the lot size. In this case, the hypergeometric sampling distribution is appropriate. A typical rule of thumb is to use the hypergeometric in cases where the anticipated sample size exceeds 5 percent of the lot size.

Let p_0 and p_1 represent the AQL and RQL, respectively, and test $H_0: p = p_0$ versus $H_1: p = p_1$. Let M represent the lot size. Define $D_0 = p_0M$ and $D_1 = p_1M$ (round to the nearest integer). The values D_0 and D_1 represent the number of nonconforming items in the lot under H_0 and H_1, respectively. Let d_k represent the number of nonconforming items found in the first k observations. The likelihood functions under H_0 and H_1 are given by

$$f_0(d_k, k) = \frac{\binom{D_0}{d_k}\binom{M - D_0}{k - d_k}}{\binom{M}{k}} \tag{4-6}$$

$$f_1(d_k, k) = \frac{\binom{D_1}{d_k}\binom{M - D_1}{k - d_k}}{\binom{M}{k}}$$

where $\binom{n}{j}$ represents a combination of n items taken j at a time

$$\binom{n}{j} = \frac{n!}{j!(n - j)!}. \tag{4-7}$$

The likelihood ratio is equal to

$$R_k = \frac{\binom{D_1}{d_k}\binom{M - D_1}{k - d_k}}{\binom{D_0}{d_k}\binom{M - D_0}{k - d_k}} \tag{4-8}$$

and the test procedure is to:

      (i) reject H_0 if $R_k > A$;
      (ii) accept H_0 if $R_k < B$; and
      (iii) continue to sample if $B \leq R_k \leq A$

where $A = (1 - \beta)/\alpha$ and $B = \beta/(1 - \alpha)$. In this case, this sequential test *cannot* be reexpressed in terms of linear boundaries for d_k. To perform the test, evaluate R_k after each observation and compare the results to the values of A and B. Alternately, accept and reject values corresponding to each value of k can be determined in advance. The reject value at step k is the smallest of the possible values of d_k (d_k ranges from 0 to k) for which R_k exceeds A, and the accept value is the largest of the possible values of d_k for which R_k is less than B.

A detailed treatment of sequential testing based on the hypergeometric distribution can be found in Meeker (1975). Topics include test plan design for one- and two-sided alternatives, truncation criteria, and estimation of the number of nonconforming items in the lot. A variety of examples are presented and programs are provided for designing and evaluating test plans.

Example 4.2:

Suppose that M = 200, p_0 = 0.05, p_1 = 0.20, and acceptable risks of Type I and Type II errors are specified as $\alpha = \beta \approx 0.10$. One possible fixed sample size plan would use sample size n = 25 and reject the lot if the sample contained three or more nonconforming items. This plan has exact error probabilities α = 0.114 and β = 0.084.

Figure 7A illustrates an alternative sequential procedure based on boundaries A = 9.2 and B = 0.05. At m_0 = 25 observations, the sequential procedure is truncated and the fixed sample size decision rule is used. This plan was chosen by calculating bounds for R_k as specified by (4-8) and the following paragraph, and then modifying these bounds to provide a better match of the OC functions for the sequential and fixed sample size procedures. The modifications were done by trial and error, with the direct method used to calculate OC function values. Since the plan of Figure 7A will inevitably reject if three nonconforming items are observed, the plan can be improved on (a reduction in ASN is achieved) by curtailing at d_k = 3. The final curtailed plan is illustrated in Figure 7B, along with a sample result and conclusion.

Figure 7A: Sequential Plan for Hypergeometric Sampling

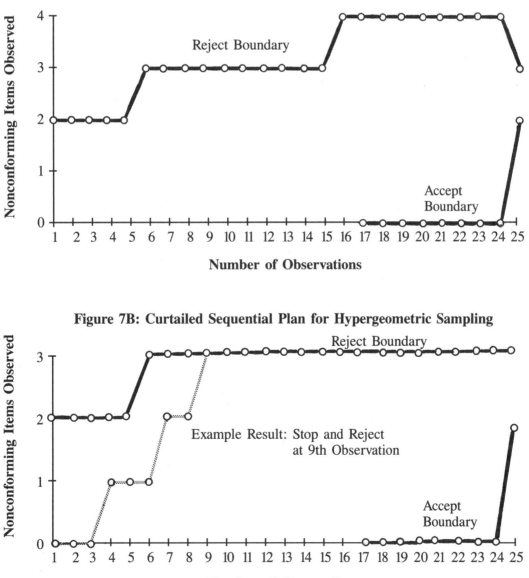

Figure 7B: Curtailed Sequential Plan for Hypergeometric Sampling

As an example of boundary determination, suppose k = 16. Calculate $D_0 = 0.05(200) = 10$ and $D_1 = 0.20(200) = 40$. At, for example, $d_{16} = 4$ calculate

$$R_k = \frac{\binom{40}{4}\binom{160}{12}}{\binom{10}{4}\binom{190}{12}} = 51.70.$$

At $d_{16} = 3$, a similar calculation yields $R_k = 8.13$. Since $8.13 < A < 51.70$, the rejection boundary at k = 16 is equal to 4. For the acceptance boundary, calculate $R_k = 0.056$ at $d_{16} = 0$. Since this value of R_k exceeds B, there is no acceptance region at this step (the best possible result, zero nonconforming items in the 16 observations, is not strong enough evidence to stop and accept the lot).

OC and ASN Function Calculations

In the case of hypergeometric sampling, Wald approximation formulas of the type presented in Section 4.1.1 (binomial sampling) and Appendix A are not available. The direct method is recommended for generating OC and ASN values. The convolution formulas involved in the direct method calculations are somewhat more complex than in the binomial example, as successive observations are not independent in the hypergeometric case (the probability of obtaining a nonconforming item on any observation depends on the number of conforming and nonconforming items remaining in the lot, which varies as the sampling process continues).

Figure 8A: OC Functions for Hypergeometric Sampling

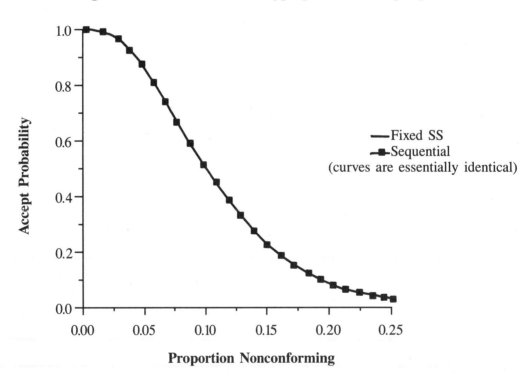

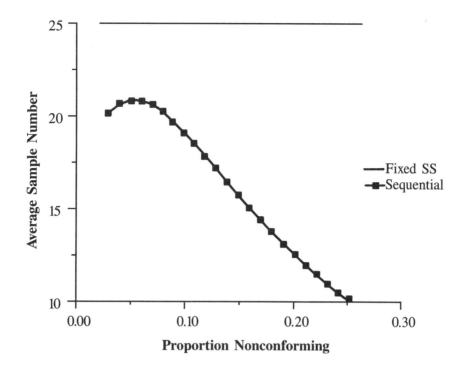

Figure 8B: ASN Functions for Hypergeometric Sampling

OC and ASN functions for Example 4.2 are plotted in Figures 8A and 8B. For practical purposes the OC functions of the sequential and fixed sample size procedures match, so the use of the sequential procedure results in no loss of ability to distinguish between acceptable and unacceptable lots. When the actual number of nonconforming items in the lot equals the AQL value of 10 (corresponding to $p_0 = 0.05$), the ASN of the sequential plan is 20.8, an average 17 percent savings over the comparable fixed sample size plan. Since the sequential plan presented here is truncated at $m_0 = 25$, there is no chance that the sequential plan will require more observations than the comparable fixed sample size plan. When the RQL value of 40 (corresponding to $p_1 = 0.20$) holds, the ASN of the sequential plan is 12.8, for an average 49 percent savings in the required number of observations.

Truncation

The hypergeometric example was arbitrarily truncated at the sample size of the comparable fixed sample size test ($m_0 = n = 25$). This truncation value is much smaller than the one calculated according to the very conservative procedure of Section 4.1.1, which would in this case truncate at $3 \cdot \max(20.8, 12.8) \approx 62$ observations. However, the use of the direct method to calculate an accurate OC function provides assurance that the truncated procedure does have acceptable operating characteristics, as illustrated in Figure 8A.

4.1.3 Poisson Sampling

Consider a situation where an item is inspected to determine the *number* of nonconformities related to the item. For example, a casting might be examined to determine the number of blemishes. In this case, the Poisson distribution is frequently used to model the distribution of X, the random number of nonconformities per item. Let λ represent the mean number of nonconformities per item, and consider testing $H_0: \lambda = \lambda_0$ versus $H_1: \lambda = \lambda_1$. Let X_i represent the number of nonconformities observed for the ith item, and let

$$c_k = \sum_{i=1}^{k} X_i, \qquad (4\text{-}9)$$

the total number of nonconformities observed in the first k items inspected. The likelihood functions under H_0 and H_1 are given by

15

$$f_0(\underline{x},k) = \{\exp(-k\lambda_0)\cdot(k\lambda_0)^{c_k}\}/(c_k!) \qquad (4\text{-}10)$$
$$f_1(\underline{x},k) = \{\exp(-k\lambda_1)\cdot(k\lambda_1)^{c_k}\}/(c_k!).$$

The likelihood ratio is equal to

$$R_k = \exp\{-k(\lambda_1 - \lambda_0)\}\cdot(\lambda_1/\lambda_0)^{c_k} \qquad (4\text{-}11)$$

and the sequential test of H_0 versus H_1 is as follows:

(i) stop and reject H_0 if $c_k > h_2 + sk$;
(ii) stop and accept H_0 if $c_k < -h_1 + sk$; and
(iii) continue to sample if $-h_1 + sk \le c_k \le h_2 + sk$

where

$$a = \ln A = \ln[(1 - \beta)/\alpha] \qquad\qquad b = -\ln B = -\ln[\beta/(1 - \alpha)] \qquad (4\text{-}12)$$
$$r = \ln(\lambda_1/\lambda_0) \qquad\qquad\qquad\qquad s = (\lambda_1 - \lambda_0)/r$$
$$h_1 = b/r \qquad\qquad\qquad\qquad\qquad h_2 = a/r.$$

Example 4.3:

Consider testing H_0: $\lambda = 1$ versus H_1: $\lambda = 2$ and suppose that Type I and Type II errors are not to exceed 0.05 and 0.10, respectively. One fixed sample size plan meeting this criteria (found from Poisson probability tables) is to take n = 13 samples and to reject H_0 if the total number of nonconformities observed is 20 or more. Otherwise, H_0 is not rejected. This plan has exact error probabilities of $\alpha = 0.0427$ and $\beta = 0.0968$.

To find a sequential procedure with approximately the same error probabilities, calculate

$$a = \ln(A) = \ln[(1 - 0.0968)/0.0427] = 3.052$$
$$b = -\ln(B) = -\ln[0.0968/(1 - 0.0427)] = 2.291$$
$$r = \ln(2/1) = 0.693$$
$$s = (2 - 1)/0.693 = 1.443$$
$$h_1 = 2.291/0.693 = 3.306$$
$$h_2 = 3.052/0.693 = 4.404.$$

The rejection and acceptance boundaries of the test are determined, respectively, by the equations

$$c_k = 4.404 + 1.443k$$
$$c_k = -3.306 + 1.443k.$$

This plan, truncated at $m_0 = 21$ observations, is illustrated in Figure 9. As in the binomial and hypergeometric examples, the truncated plan is curtailed as soon as the reject decision becomes inevitable.

Figure 9: Sequential Test Plan for Poisson Sampling

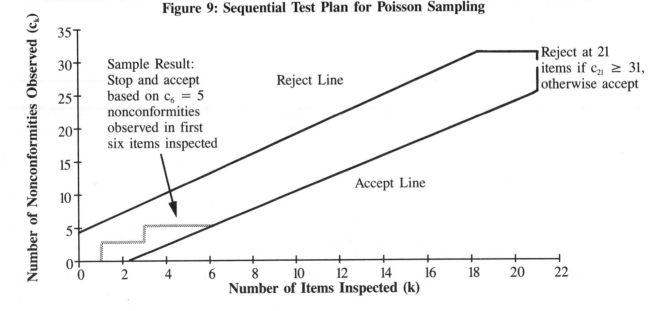

OC and ASN Function Calculations

Five points on the OC and ASN functions can be quickly calculated:

λ	$P_A(\lambda)$	$ASN\ (\lambda)$	
$\lambda = 0.0$	1.0	$[[h_1/s]] + 1$	(4-13)
$\lambda = \lambda_0$	$\approx 1 - \alpha$	$\approx [(1 - \alpha)h_1 - \alpha\ h_2] / [s - \lambda_0]$	
$\lambda = s$	$\approx h_2/(h_1 + h_2)$	$\approx h_1 h_2/s$	
$\lambda = \lambda_1$	$\approx \beta$	$\approx [(1 - \beta)\ h_2 - \beta\ h_1] / [\lambda_1 - s]$	
$\lambda \rightarrow \infty$	0.0	$0*$	

Rough sketches of the OC or ASN function can be obtained by connecting these five points. As in the binomial case, these formulas represent specific results from a general approximation procedure which is described in Appendix A.

The direct method (Section 5) can be used to calculate exact OC and ASN function values. The program required in the case of Poisson sampling is considerably longer than the one used in the binomial example, and is not presented in this text. Using this method, calculated error probabilities for the sequential test (with no truncation) are $\alpha = 0.024$ and $\beta = 0.071$. The goal of matching the fixed sample size test values of 0.043 and 0.097 has been more than satisfied, as the test is quite conservative at both λ_0 and λ_1. At $\lambda = \lambda_0 = 1.0$ the ASN is 8.19 with a standard deviation of 5.63. The probability of exceeding the fixed sample size test value of n = 13 is equal to 0.14. If λ *is* equal to 1.0, the use of the sequential rather than the fixed sample procedure will save, on the average, about five observations. The sequential plan will require *more* than 13 observations about 14 percent of the time, so the savings is *not* guaranteed. At $\lambda = \lambda_1 = 2.0$, the ASN is 8.72 with a standard deviation of 6.07. The probability of needing more than 13 observations to complete the test is equal to 0.18. The "worst case" occurs around $\lambda = 1.5$, where the ASN equals 14.12 with a standard deviation of 11.45. At this value of λ, more than 13 observations would be required about 39 percent of the time. In this example we see a situation where the use of the sequential procedure could *increase* the expected number of observations required. This is due to the conservative nature of this sequential test (both α and β are considerably less than the corresponding fixed sample size test values).

Using the direct method and simple search techniques, the boundaries of the sequential test procedure were modified in order to match more closely the fixed sample size test's error probabilities. It was determined that the test having rejection and acceptance boundaries determined, respectively, by the equations

$$c_k = 3.6 + 1.443k$$
$$c_k = -2.8 + 1.443k$$

has exact error probabilities $\alpha = 0.042$ and $\beta = 0.096$, which are quite close to the fixed sample size test values of 0.043 and 0.097. This modified procedure has ASN values of 6.92 at $\lambda = \lambda_0 = 1.0$; 7.04 at $\lambda = \lambda_1 = 2.0$; and 10.52 at $\lambda = 1.5$. A savings (compared to the fixed sample size plan value of n = 13) in expected sample size is now achieved for *all* possible values of λ.

Truncation

As in the binomial example, a conservative truncation procedure can be used to ensure that the sequential test will not require an unreasonable number of observations. Truncating the modified sequential plan at $3 \cdot (max\{ASN(\lambda_0), ASN(\lambda_1)\}) = 3 \cdot (max\{6.92, 7.04\}) \approx 21$ observations will have no real impact on the OC function, will further reduce the ASN for the "middle" values of λ, and will provide protection against the occurrence of large sample sizes. If a decision has not been reached by the 21st observation, the process stops and the decision is made according to which boundary the point (k, c_k) lies closest.

---

*The rejection number is reached before the first unit is completely inspected.

Figure 10A: OC Functions for Poisson Sampling

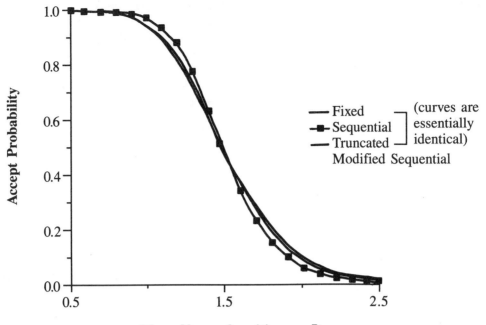

Figure 10B: ASN Functions for Poisson Sampling

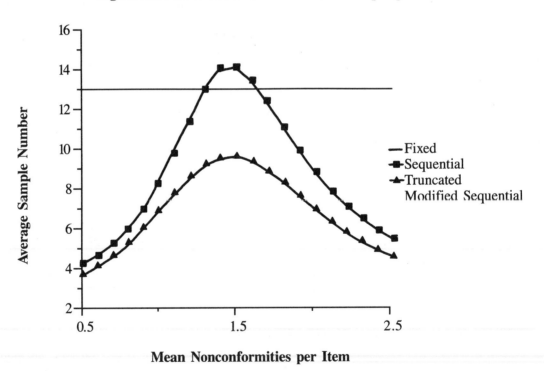

Figures 10A and 10B show OC and ASN functions for the fixed sample size, sequential, and modified truncated sequential plans. The final modified truncated plan has virtually the same OC function as the fixed sample size plan and results in a substantial savings in the expected number of required observations.

4.1.4 Comparative Binomial Trials

Let π_1 and π_2 represent the "success" probabilities for two binomial distributions, and consider the problem of testing H_0: $\pi_1 = \pi_2$ versus H_1: $\pi_1 \neq \pi_2$. This problem is of particular interest when considering clinical trials, where π_1 might represent the probability of a patient's recovery when subjected to Treatment 1 while π_2 represents the probability of recovery under Treatment 2. If a serious illness is being treated then sequential test procedures are particularly valuable for ethical reasons: If one treatment is superior to the other, the doctor in charge of the trials would want to discover this as soon as possible so that all patients could be given the better treatment.

An appropriate truncated sequential procedure is given by Armitage (1957). Although the procedure is motivated by a medical application, it would be equally useful in an industrial setting whenever the goal is to compare two "success" rates. The procedure is based on pairing the subjects and randomly selecting one member of each pair to receive Treatment 1, with the other receiving Treatment 2. Results are classified three ways: A tie occurs if either both treatments are successful or both are failures; a type "FS" result occurs if Treatment 1 fails while Treatment 2 is successful; and a type "SF" result occurs if Treatment 1 is successful while Treatment 2 fails. Ties are ignored and the test statistic, based on observing k *untied* pairs, is given by $y_k = n_{1k} - n_{2k}$. The terms n_{1k} and n_{2k} represent the number of FS and SF results, respectively, observed in the k untied pairs. The null hypothesis is reexpressed in terms of three alternatives for the probability θ that an untied pair is an FS

$$H_0: \theta = 1/2 \text{ versus } H_+: \theta = \theta_1 \text{ versus } H_-: \theta = 1 - \theta_1$$

where $\theta_1 > 1/2$. If $\theta = 1/2$ then FS and SF are equally likely and the treatments are considered to be equally effective. A value of θ greater (less) than 1/2 indicates that Treatment 2 is more (less) effective than Treatment 1.

To construct a sequential test having error probabilities 2α and β, a Wald-style upper reject boundary is determined as usual by setting the likelihood ratio equal to A and then expressing the result as a linear function of k. The lower reject boundary is just the reflection of the upper boundary about the horizontal axis. Instead of choosing accept boundaries in the usual manner, Armitage's procedure selects the truncation value m_0 and accepts H_0 if as of the m_0th untied pair neither reject boundary has been reached. The procedure is summarized as follows:

    (i) stop and reject H_0 in favor of H_+ if $y_k > a + bk$;
    (ii) stop and reject H_0 in favor of H_- if $y_k < -a - bk$; and
    (iii) continue to sample if $-a - bk \leq y_k \leq a + bk$. If $k = m_0$ and (i) or (ii) do not hold, stop, and accept.

Parameters a and b are calculated according to

$$a = \frac{2 \log\{(1 - \beta)/\alpha\}}{\log\{\theta_1/(1 - \theta_1)\}} \qquad b = \frac{2 \log\{\theta_1^{-1/2}(1 - \theta_1)^{-1/2}/2\}}{\log\{\theta_1/(1 - \theta_1)\}}. \qquad (4\text{-}14)$$

The truncation value m_0 which leads to specified error probabilities 2α and β is more difficult to determine. Armitage (1957) gives a formula for approximating m_0 and a table of values of a, b, and m_0 when $2\alpha = \beta = 0.05$. Armitage's primary results are reproduced in Table 3.

Table 3: Sequential Test Plans for Comparing Proportions*

$$\alpha = 0.025 \qquad \beta = 0.05$$

| | Test Plan Parameters | | Truncation Value | |
θ_1	a	b	m_0	Fixed Sample Size**
0.55	36.25	0.0501	1778	1294
0.60	17.94	0.1007	439	319
0.65	11.75	0.1524	191	138
0.70	8.59	0.2058	104	75
0.75	6.62	0.2619	66	46
0.80	5.25	0.3219	44	30
0.85	4.19	0.3882	30	20
0.90	3.31	0.4650	22	14
0.95	2.47	0.5640	15	9

*From "Restricted Sequential Procedures" by Armitage (1957). Reproduced by permission of the Biometrika Trustees.

**Fixed sample size required to match the OC function of the sequential plan.

Example 4.4:

Suppose that $\theta_1 = 0.8$, $\alpha = 0.025$ and $\beta = 0.05$. From formulas (4-14) or Table 3 obtain $a = 5.25$ and $b = 0.3219$. Table 3 gives the truncation value $m_0 = 44$. An approximately equivalent fixed sample size test requires $N = 30$ untied observations, rejects H_0 in favor of H_+ if $y_{30} > 11$, rejects H_0 in favor of H_- if $y_{30} < -11$, and accepts H_0 if $-11 \leq y_{30} \leq 11$.

Figure 11A: Sequential Test Plan for Comparing Proportions

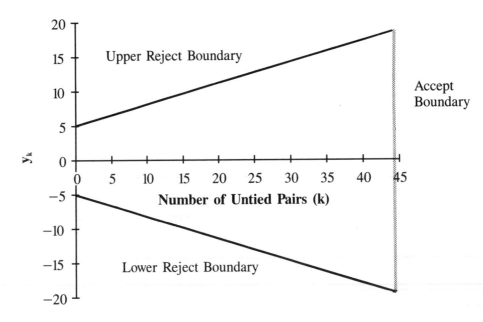

Figure 11B: Curtailed Sequential Test Plan for Comparing Proportions

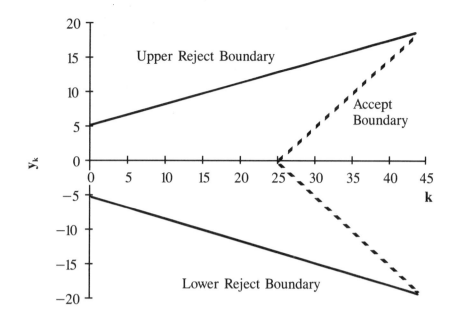

The truncated sequential test is shown in Figure 11A. Figure 11B shows a modified version of the test where the process is curtailed as soon as the accept decision becomes inevitable. Although Armitage gives an approximation formula for the OC function, OC and ASN values are best calculated using the direct method. Figures 12A and 12B illustrate the OC and ASN functions, respectively, for the curtailed sequential and fixed sample size test procedures. The OC curves are seen to be functionally equivalent, while the ASN functions show a substantial savings in the expected number of required observations when either treatment is substantially better. Note that when θ is near 1/2 (the H_0 value) the sequential and fixed sample size procedures require, on average, approximately the same number of observations so no savings can be expected from the use of the sequential procedure. This is a function of the shape of the accept region and relates to the ethical considerations which motivated the sequential procedure. If θ is near 1/2 then the treatments are equally effective and there is no motivation to reduce the number of required observations, while θ-values far from 1/2 should result in a quick conclusion. Therefore, the test is designed to have low ASN values when θ is far from 1/2 with less concern for the ASN when θ is near 1/2.

Figure 12A: OC Functions for Comparing Two Proportions

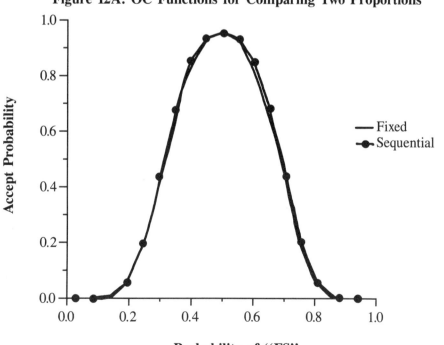

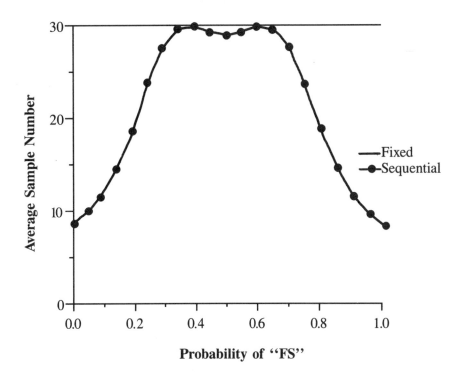

Figure 12B: ASN Functions for Comparing Two Proportions

Although Armitage's procedure is truncated at a specified value m_0, there is no guarantee that only m_0 observations will be required since the test ignores tied pairs and must continue until, at most, m_0 *untied* pairs are obtained. Aroian and Oksoy (1975) present a truncated test which uses ties as well as untied pairs, providing an absolute upper bound on the number of required observations.

This example is only one of a broad collection of applications of sequential methods to medical trials. Armitage (1975) devotes an entire text to the subject. Other recent results can be found in Hearron, et al (1984).

4.2 Variables Sampling

4.2.1 Tests Involving a Process Mean

Standard Deviation (σ) Known

In this example, values of a normally distributed variable X with unknown mean μ and known standard deviation σ are observed. Consider a test designed to detect an *increase* in the mean of the distribution

$$H_0: \mu = \mu_0 \text{ versus } H_1: \mu = \mu_1 \text{ where } \mu_1 > \mu_0.$$

Let X_i represent the value of the ith measurement, and let

$$S_k = \sum_{i=1}^{k} X_i. \tag{4-15}$$

As in the previous examples, the test based on the likelihood ratio can be expressed in terms of linear boundaries:

(i) stop and reject H_0 if $S_k > h_2 + sk$;
(ii) stop and accept H_0 if $S_k < -h_1 + sk$; and
(iii) continue to sample if $-h_1 + sk \leq S_k \leq h_2 + sk$

where

$$s = (\mu_0 + \mu_1)/2 \qquad\qquad h_1 = (\sigma^2 b)/(\mu_1 - \mu_0) \qquad (4\text{-}16)$$
$$a = \ln A = \ln\{(1 - \beta)/\alpha\} \qquad h_2 = (\sigma^2 a)/(\mu_1 - \mu_0).$$
$$b = -\ln B = \ln\{(1 - \alpha)/\beta\}$$

Example 4.5:

When in control, a process mean is known to equal $\mu = 20$ mm. Consider testing H_0: $\mu = 20$ versus H_1: $\mu = 20.5$ based on observations from a normal distribution with standard deviation $\sigma = 1.0$ mm. If error probabilities $\alpha = 0.05$ and $\beta = 0.10$ are specified, then the appropriate fixed sample size test requires approximately 35 observations. This test rejects H_0 if the sample mean exceeds 20.28. To find the corresponding sequential test, use equations (4-16) to calculate

$$s = 20.25 \qquad h_1 = 4.50 \qquad h_2 = 5.78$$

so the sequential test would reject at the kth observation if $S_k > 5.78 + 20.25k$; accept at the kth observation if $S_k < -4.50 + 20.25k$; and continue to sample otherwise. Alternatively, reject if $\overline{X}_k > 20.25 + 5.78/k$ and accept if $\overline{X}_k < 20.25 - 4.5/k$. This test is presented graphically in Figure 13. The inspector need only plot the point (k, S_k) after each observation is made to determine whether to stop and reject, stop and accept, or make another observation.

Figure 13: Sequential Test Plan, Variables Sampling

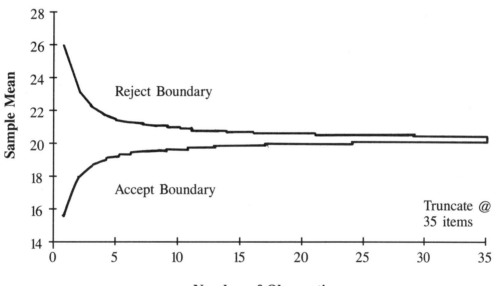

Number of Observations

To detect a *decrease* in the process mean, the hypothesis test specification is

$$H_0: \mu = \mu_0 \text{ versus } H_1: \mu = \mu_1 \text{ where } \mu_1 < \mu_0.$$

In this case formulas (4-16) are still used, but the test criteria is to:

    (i) stop and accept H_0 if $S_k > -h_1 + sk$ (h_1 and h_2 will have negative values);
    (ii) stop and reject H_0 if $S_k < h_2 + sk$; and
    (iii) continue to sample if $h_2 + sk \leq S_k \leq -h_1 + sk$.

For example, consider testing H_0: $\mu = 20.0$ versus H_1:$\mu = 19.5$ where $\sigma = 1.0$, $\alpha = 0.05$, and $\beta = 0.10$. Calculate $s = 19.75$, $h_1 = -4.50$, and $h_2 = -5.78$. The sequential test plan is to stop and reject at the kth observation if $S_k < -5.78 + 19.75k$; stop and accept if $S_k > 4.50 + 19.75k$; and continue to sample otherwise.

    An approximate *two-sided* test can be performed by combining two one-sided tests in the manner shown in the sequential t-test section. This is most easily done if the test criteria are reexpressed in terms of total deviation from μ_0. The one-sided test of the preceding paragraph can be expressed as:

> (i) stop and accept H_0 if $\Sigma (X_i - 20) > 4.50 - 0.25k$;
> (ii) stop and reject H_0 if $\Sigma (X_i - 20) < -5.78 - 0.25 k$; and
> (iii) continue to sample if $-5.78 - 0.25k \le S_k \le 4.50 - 0.25k$.

Armitage (1957) contains a detailed presentation of truncated two-sided tests.

OC and ASN Function Calculations

Five points on the OC and ASN curves can be easily *approximated:*

μ	$P_A(\mu)$	$ASN(\mu)$	
$\mu << \mu_0$	1.0	1.0	(4-17)
$\mu = \mu_0$	$\approx 1 - \alpha$	$\approx [(1 - \alpha) h_1 - \alpha h_2] / [s - \mu_0]$	
$\mu = s$	$\approx h_2/(h_1 + h_2)$	$\approx h_1 h_2/\sigma^2$	
$\mu = \mu_1$	$\approx \beta$	$\approx [(1 - \beta) h_2 - \beta h_1] / [\mu_1 - s]$	
$\mu >> \mu_1$	0.0	1.0.	

In Example 4.5, at $\mu = \mu_0 = 20.0$, $ASN(\mu) \approx 16.0$. At $\mu = s = 20.25$, $P_A(\mu) \approx 0.56$ and $ASN (\mu) \approx 26.0$. At $\mu = \mu_1 = 20.5$, $ASN (\mu) \approx 19.0$. The ASN values compare favorably with the 35 observations required for the fixed sample size test. A rough sketch of the OC or ASN function can be obtained by plotting and connecting the five points. More general formulas for approximating OC and ASN values at any value of μ can be found in Appendix A.

The direct method can also be used to calculate exact OC and ASN values in this example. In the case of sampling by variables (from a continuous distribution), a complex program is required which must numerically integrate a sequence of continuous conditional density functions. The direct method was used to calculate values plotted in Figures 14A and 14B which show OC and ASN functions for the fixed sample size and sequential test plans. The figures show a substantial improvement in the expected number of observations required to reach a decision, with no degradation of the OC function.

Figure 14A: OC Functions, Testing for Process Mean

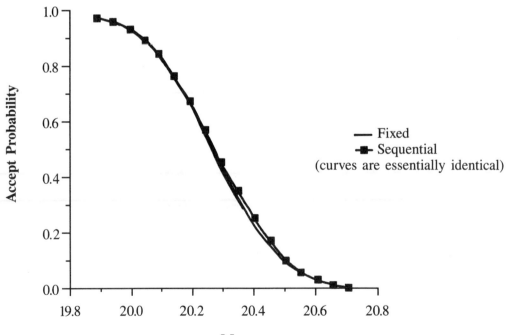

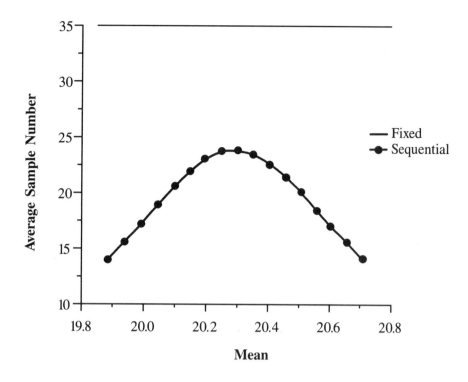

Figure 14B: ASN Functions, Testing for Process Mean

A third approach to OC and ASN calculation is to perform a simulation (Monte Carlo) study. Although not as precise as a well-written direct method routine, a simulation study based on a large sample size could yield adequate precision and would be considerably easier to program. In addition, Aroian and Robison (1969) give tables of OC and ASN values for a variety of one-sided sequential tests.

Standard Deviation (σ) Unknown: Sequential t-Test

Consider Example 4.5, but suppose that the standard deviation σ is unknown. In this case the sequential t-test is appropriate. The mathematics underlying the sequential t-test are quite complex, and simple formulas for test boundaries are not available. There are several sources of tables. Suich and Iglewicz (1970) give tables of boundaries for truncated t-tests in the case where $\alpha = \beta$, and Alexander and Suich (1973) treat cases where $\alpha \neq \beta$. The hypothesis test is expressed in terms of the size of shift in the process mean which the test is designed to detect, expressed in standard deviation units. An example formulation for a one-sided test is

$$H_0: \delta = 0 \text{ versus } H_1: \delta > 0$$

where $\delta = (\mu_1 - \mu_0)/\sigma$. Alexander and Suich's tables are indexed by α, β, and δ. The most convenient form of the sequential t-test statistic is

$$U_k = \frac{\displaystyle\sum_{i=1}^{k} (X_i - \mu_0)}{\sqrt{\displaystyle\sum_{i=1}^{k} (X_i - \mu_0)^2}} \tag{4-18}$$

where μ_0 represents the in-control process mean.

Example 4.6:

Suppose that a process has in-control mean $\mu_0 = 20.0$ and we wish to detect an increase in the mean of $\delta = 0.5$ standard deviations with probability $1 - \beta = 0.90$. This test of H_0: $\delta = 0$ versus H_1: $\delta > 0$ would be equivalent to the test performed in Example 4.5 if the standard deviation were indeed 1.0. Table 4 gives boundaries for an appropriate truncated sequential t-test based on $\alpha = 0.05$, $\beta = 0.10$. Figure 15 illustrates the test graphically, along with a typical sample result leading to rejection of H_0.

Table 4: Truncated Sequential t-test Boundaries*

$\alpha = .05, \beta = .10, \delta = .5$

k	$\Phi_L(U_k)$**	$\Phi_u(U_k)$***	k	$\Phi_L(U_k)$	$\Phi_u(U_k)$
5	-2.079	-	25	.519	2.314
6	-1.782	-	30	.768	2.268
7	-1.382	-	35	.982	2.268
8	-1.144	-	40	1.172	2.229
10	-.799	2.793	45	1.342	2.226
12	-.512	2.665	50	1.498	2.229
14	-.279	2.570	55	1.643	2.237
16	-.091	2.496	65	1.915	2.263
18	.071	2.438	75	2.140	2.297
20	.215	2.393	84	2.332	2.333

$\Phi_0 = 2.333$[†]

$\alpha = .025, \beta = .05, \delta = 1.0$

k	$\Phi_L(U_k)$	$\Phi_u(U_k)$	k	$\Phi_L(U_k)$	$\Phi_u(U_k)$
3	-1.483	-	12	1.091	2.263
4	-.757	-	14	1.428	2.263
5	-.313	-	16	1.537	2.271
6	.008	2.379	18	1.726	2.285
7	.261	2.449	20	1.898	2.304
8	.471	2.310	22	2.058	2.325
9	.653	2.290	24	2.207	2.349
10	.814	2.276	26	2.348	2.374

$\Phi_0 = 2.402$

*Adapted from "A Truncated Sequential t-Test for General α and β" by Alexander and Suich (1973), with permission from the American Statistical Association.

**Accept boundary value.

***Reject boundary value.

† Truncation criteria. If the maximum tabulated value for k (84 in the first example) is reached, accept H_0 if $U_k \leq \Phi_0$, otherwise reject.

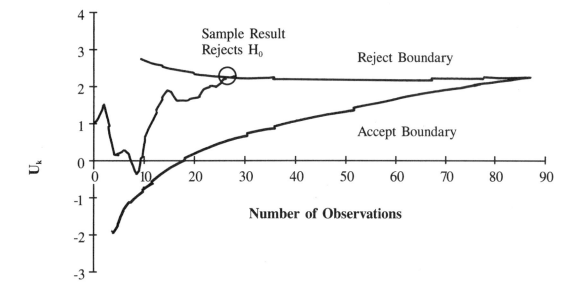

The mathematics involved in the calculation of OC and ASN function values are prohibitive for sequential t-tests, so simulation (Monte Carlo) studies are typically performed. Studies performed by Alexander and Suich (1973) demonstrate the typical advantages of sequential procedures: there is good agreement with the specified α and β values and substantial savings are realized in terms of the expected number of observations required to confidently reach a conclusion.

The sequential t-test can easily be modified to handle "less than" alternatives and two-sided alternatives. To test H_0: $\delta = 0$ versus H_1: $\delta < 0$ simply reverse the signs of Alexander and Suich's boundaries. To test H_0: $\delta = 0$ versus H_1: $\delta \neq 0$ at specified levels of α and β, the scheme is slightly more complex. Perform two simultaneous one-sided tests, each at levels $\alpha' = \alpha/2$ and β. Figure 16 illustrates a sequential t-test designed to detect a $\delta = 1.0$ standard deviation shift in the process mean, based on $\alpha = 0.05$ and $\beta = 0.05$. Test boundaries are from Table 4, with $\alpha' = 0.05/2 = 0.025$ and $\beta = 0.05$. As the figure indicates, overlapping boundaries are simply ignored.

Figure 16: Two-Sided Truncated Sequential t-test

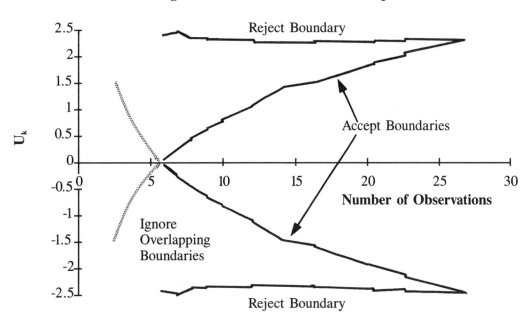

4.2.2 Tests Involving Process Variability

In this example, values of a normally distributed variable X with mean μ (assumed to be known) and unknown standard deviation σ are observed. Consider a test designed to detect an *increase* in process variability

$$H_0: \sigma = \sigma_0 \text{ versus } H_1: \sigma = \sigma_1 \text{ where } \sigma_1 > \sigma_0.$$

Let X_i represent the value of the ith measurement, and let

$$T_k = \sum_{i=1}^{k} (X_i - \mu)^2. \tag{4-19}$$

Once again, the test based on the likelihood ratio can be expressed in terms of linear boundaries:

(i) stop and reject H_0 if $T_k > h_2 + sk$;
(ii) stop and accept H_0 if $T_k < -h_1 + sk$; and
(iii) continue to sample if $-h_1 + sk \le T_k \le h_2 + sk$

where

$$\begin{array}{ll}
s = \ln(\sigma_1^2/\sigma_0^2)/(1/\sigma_0^2 - 1/\sigma_1^2) & h_1 = 2b/(1/\sigma_0^2 - 1/\sigma_1^2) \\
a = \ln A = \ln\{(1 - \beta)/\alpha\} & h_2 = 2a/(1/\sigma_0^2 - 1/\sigma_1^2). \\
b = -\ln B = \ln\{(1 - \alpha)/\beta\} &
\end{array} \tag{4-20}$$

Example 4.7:

When in control a process is known to have standard deviation $\sigma = 0.10$ oz. Consider testing $H_0: \sigma = 0.10$ versus $H_1: \sigma = 0.15$ based on observations from a normal distribution with mean $\mu = 16$ oz. If error probabilities $\alpha = 0.10$ and $\beta = 0.05$ are specified, then the appropriate fixed sample size test requires $n = 28$ observations. This test rejects H_0 if T_n/σ_0^2 exceeds 37.92. To find the corresponding sequential test, use equations (4-20) to calculate

$$s = 0.0146 \qquad h_1 = 0.1041 \qquad h_2 = 0.0810$$

so the sequential test would reject at the kth observation if $T_k > 0.08102 + 0.0146k$; accept at the kth observation if $T_k < -0.1041 + 0.0146k$; and continue to sample otherwise.

OC and ASN Function Calculations

Five points on the OC and ASN curves can be easily calculated:

σ	$P_A(\sigma)$	$ASN(\sigma)$	
$\sigma = 0$	1.0	$[[h_2/s]] + 1$	(4-21)
$\sigma = \sigma_0$	$\approx 1 - \alpha$	$\approx [(1 - \alpha) h_1 - \alpha h_2] / [s - \sigma_0^2]$	
$\sigma = \sqrt{s}$	$\approx h_2/(h_1 + h_2)$	$\approx h_1 h_2/2s^2$	
$\sigma = \sigma_1$	$\approx \beta$	$\approx [(1 - \beta) h_2 - \beta h_1] / [\sigma_1^2 - s]$	
$\sigma >> \sigma_1$	0.0	1.0.	

In Example 4.7, at $\sigma = \sigma_0 = 0.10$, $ASN(\sigma) \approx 18.6$. At $\sigma = \sqrt{s} = 0.121$, $P_A(\sigma) \approx 0.44$ and $ASN(\sigma) \approx 19.8$. At $\sigma = \sigma_1 = 0.15$, $ASN(\sigma) \approx 9.1$. The ASN values compare favorably with the 28 observations required for the fixed sample size test. The savings realized by using the sequential procedure is particularly impressive in the case where H_1 is true.

A rough sketch of the OC or ASN function can be obtained by plotting and connecting the five points. As in previous examples, formulas for approximating OC and ASN values at any value of σ can be found in Appendix A. The direct method or simulation techniques should be used if more accurate OC or ASN values are desired.

Figure 17A: OC Functions, Testing for Process Variability

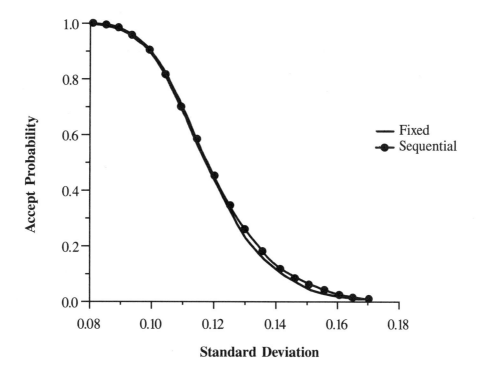

Figure 17B: ASN Functions, Testing for Process Variability

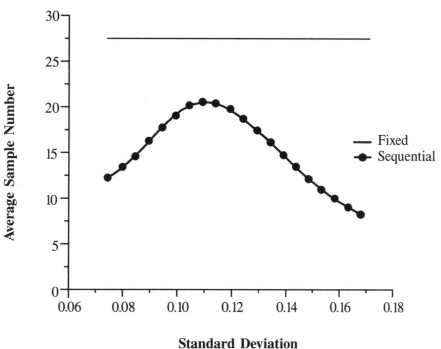

Figures 17A and 17B illustrate OC and ASN functions for the test plan of Example 4.7. The plan was arbitrarily truncated at the fixed sample size value: $m_0 = n = 28$. The plots, based on direct method calculations, show that this aggressive truncation scheme has no real impact on the plan's OC function while achieving a substantial reduction in the number of required observations.

The test is of course limited in application to situations where the process mean μ is known. For tests involving the variance of a process having an unknown mean, refer to Goss (1973).

4.3 Sequential Life Testing

Consider testing:

$$H_0: \theta = \theta_0 \text{ versus } H_1: \theta = \theta_1 \qquad \theta_0 > \theta_1$$

where the parameter θ represents the mean lifetime of a product. Typically, the exponential distribution is used to model the random lifetime of the product. Suppose that, at time zero, n items are put on test (testing may be done with or without replacement). Let $V(t)$ represent the total time on test as of time t, and let $r(t)$ represent the number of observed failures. The likelihood ratio at time t is given by

$$R(t) = \{\theta_0^{r(t)}\exp(-V(t)/\theta_1)\} / \{\theta_1^{r(t)}\exp(-V(t)/\theta_0)\} \qquad (4\text{-}22)$$

and a sequential test based on Wald theory is defined as follows:

(i) stop and reject H_0 if $V(t) < -h_2 + sr(t)$;
(ii) stop and accept H_0 if $V(t) > h_1 + sr(t)$; and
(iii) continue testing if $-h_2 + sr(t) \le V(t) \le h_1 + sr(t)$.

Test parameters are calculated from

$$
\begin{aligned}
s &= \ln(\theta_0/\theta_1)/(1/\theta_1 - 1/\theta_0) \qquad (4\text{-}23)\\
h_1 &= -\ln(B)/(1/\theta_1 - 1/\theta_0) = -\ln[\beta/(1-\alpha)]/(1/\theta_1 - 1/\theta_0)\\
h_2 &= \ln(A)/(1/\theta_1 - 1/\theta_0) = \ln[(1-\beta)/\alpha]/(1/\theta_1 - 1/\theta_0).
\end{aligned}
$$

Examples of specific sequential life testing plans can be found in MIL-STD-781C (1977), along with plots of OC and average total time on test functions. The MIL-STD-781C plans are discussed in Grant and Leavenworth (1980). Schmee (1980) presents techniques for confidence interval estimation of mean lifetime following the sequential life test.

Example 4.8:

Epstein and Sobel (1955) consider testing $H_0: \theta = 7500$ hours versus $H_1: \theta = 2,500$ hours with specified error probabilities $\alpha = \beta = 0.05$. At time $t = 0$, $n = 100$ items are put on test. Testing is done with replacement, so in this case $V(t) = 100t$. An example of a fixed-length test having the specified error probabilities would be to test for 407.5 hours (or 40750 hours of total time on test) or until the 10th failure occurs. If the 10th failure occurs first, the null hypothesis is rejected. Otherwise, it is accepted. (This test is time censored when the null hypothesis is accepted, failure censored when rejected.) Note that, as in the Wald-style sequential test, the time required to reach a decision is random, since the test will not continue for the entire 407.5 hours if 10 failures are observed.

Using Formulas (4-23), the sequential test plan parameters are: $s = 4120$, $h_1 = 11042$, and $h_2 = 11042$. This test plan is presented in Figure 18A. Figure 18B shows the use of the plan when failures occur at total time on test values $V(t) = 8000$, 13000, and 18000. At time $V(t) = 23,402$ the accept boundary is reached and the test terminates. In Figure 18C, failures occur at times $V(t) = 2000$, 4000, 4800, 6200, and 7200. At the 5th failure the reject boundary is reached and the test terminates.

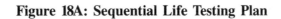

Figure 18A: Sequential Life Testing Plan

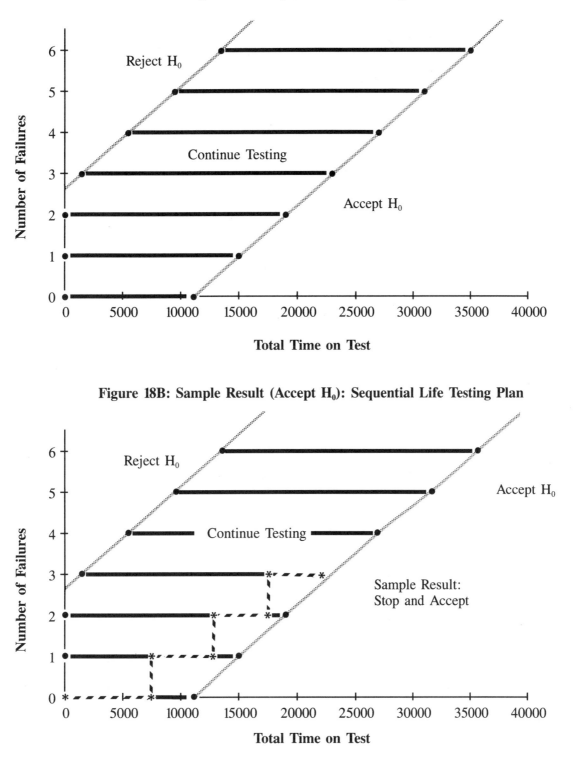

Total Time on Test

Figure 18C: Sample Result (Reject H₀): Sequential Life Testing Plan

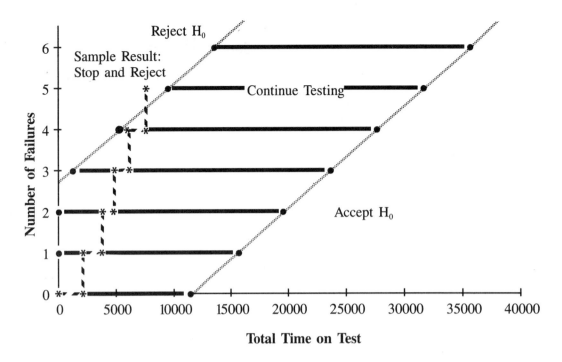

OC and ATT Function Calculations

In the case of life testing, the ASN function is replaced by the ATT (average time on test) or MET (median time to decision) functions. ATT values are expressed in total time on test units.

Five points on the OC and ATT curves can quickly be calculated:

θ	$P_A(\theta)$	$ATT(\theta)$	
$\theta \rightarrow \infty$	1.0	h_1	(4-24)
$\theta = \theta_0$	$\approx 1 - \alpha.$	$\approx \theta_0[(1-\alpha)\ln B + \alpha \ln A]/[\ln k - (k-1)]$	
$\theta = s$	$\approx \ln A/(\ln A - \ln B)$	$\approx h_1 h_2/s$	
$\theta = \theta_1$	$\approx \beta$	$\approx \theta_1[\beta\ln B + (1-\beta)\ln A]/[\ln k - (k-1)/k]$	
$\theta = 0$	0.0	0	

where $k = \theta_0/\theta_1$.

In the previous example, at $\theta = \theta_0 = 7500$, $ATT(\theta) \approx 22049$. At $\theta = s = 4120$, $P_A(\theta) \approx 0.5$ and $ATT(\theta) \approx 29594$. At $\theta = \theta_1 = 2500$, $ATT(\theta) \approx 15337$. Rough sketches of the complete OC and ATT functions can be obtained by plotting and connecting these five points. Appendix A contains formulas for approximating OC and ATT values at any value of θ.

Exact formulas for calculating OC and ATT functions are referenced in Epstein and Sobel (1955) for nontruncated testing and in Woodall and Kurkjian (1962) for truncated testing. In addition, the direct method or simulation can be used to calculate OC and ATT functions. For Epstein and Sobel's example, OC and ATT functions generated using the direct method are shown in Figures 19A and 19B. Epstein and Sobel point out that the test determined by Wald's formulas is quite conservative with respect to Type I errors, giving a true α value of 0.032 rather than 0.05 (at the expense of an increase in the ATT). They determine that the test defined by s = 4120, h_1 = 11042, and h_2 = 9690 has true error probabilities $\alpha = \beta = 0.05$ exactly. The OC and ATT functions for this test are also included in Figures 19A and 19B. Both sequential procedures result in a substantial savings in ATT over the fixed length procedure, while maintaining similar OC functions.

Figure 19A: OC Functions, Life Testing

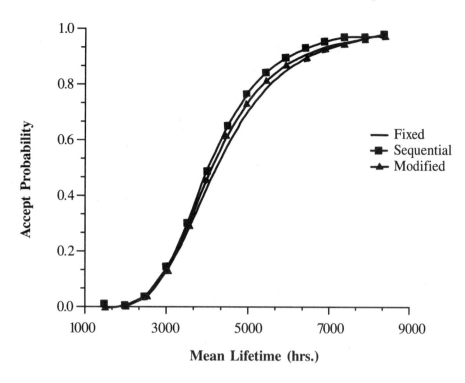

Figure 19B: Expected Time on Test, Life Testing

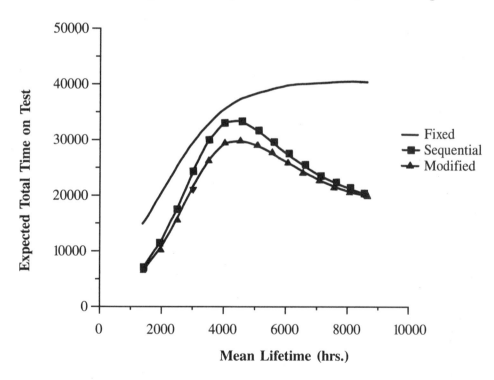

Truncation

To ensure that the sequential test will not take an unreasonable amount of time, the test can be truncated at any desired point. A truncation rule is specified by total time on test and rejection values (V_0, i_0). If total time on test V_0 is reached, the null hypothesis is rejected if i_0 or more failures have been observed, accepted otherwise. Epstein (1958) suggests choosing V_0 and i_0 to satisfy the relation $V_0 = i_0 s$. For any proposed truncation scheme, the direct method or Woodall and Kurkjian's formulas can be used to evaluate the OC and ATT functions.

5. Direct Method of Calculating OC and ASN Functions

The approximation formulas given throughout Section 4 and Appendix A for calculating OC and ASN values are appealing in terms of computational simplicity, but have several drawbacks. The numerical examples show that the approximations are not necessarily close to the exact values. In addition, the formulas were developed assuming that truncation is not implemented, and cannot be easily altered to allow for truncated plans. This leads to the conservative recommendations regarding truncation: *If* exact OC calculations are not performed, then the truncation value should be quite large to ensure that the OC function is not seriously degraded.

The direct method, developed by Aroian (1968), provides a method of computing *exact* OC and ASN values. Although computationally complex, it has several significant advantages over the approximation formulas. Exact values can be calculated for sequential plans truncated at any sample size, so the effect of incorporating truncation can be investigated. If the linear boundaries provided by Wald's formulas do not yield an acceptable OC function, the boundaries can be altered until the OC function is acceptable, using the direct method to calculate function values for any set of proposed boundaries. In addition, the direct method does *not* assume that linear boundaries are used, but allows the construction of *any* form of acceptance and rejection boundary regions.

Figure 20: Direct Method Flowchart

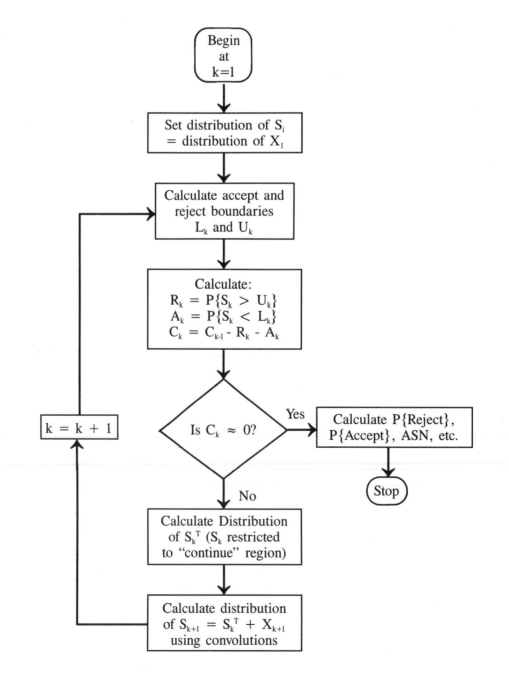

The direct method is an iterative procedure which calculates the exact distribution of the test statistic at each stage of the sampling process. A flowchart can be found in Figure 20. As an example, assume that observations are denoted $X_1, X_2, \ldots$ and that the test statistic is given by

$$S_k = \sum_{i=1}^{k} X_i. \tag{5-1}$$

Let U_k and L_k represent the step k rejection and acceptance boundaries, respectively (assume that the test stops and rejects H_0 if $S_k > U_k$, stops and accepts H_0 if $S_k < L_k$, and continues otherwise). Let R_k represent the probability that the test stops and rejects H_0 at step k: $R_k = P\{S_k > U_k\}$; and let A_k represent the probability that the test stops and accepts H_0 at step k: $A_k = P\{S_k < L_k\}$. Let C_k represent the probability of continuing beyond step k: $C_k = C_{k-1} - R_k - A_k$ (C_0 is initialized at 1.0). At the first step, $S_1 = X_1$ so the distribution of S_1 is the same as that of X_1. This distribution is used to calculate R_1, A_1, and C_1. Now consider values of S_1 truncated to this continuation region. Let S_1^T represent this restricted random variable and assign to S_1^T the truncated distribution of S_1.

To begin the iterative process, note that $S_2 = S_1^T + X_2$. The exact distribution of S_2 is found by convoluting the distributions of the independent random variables S_1^T and X_2. Once this distribution is obtained, R_2, A_2, and C_2 are calculated. The distribution of S_2^T (S_2 restricted to the continuation region) is the truncated distribution of S_2. The exact distribution of $S_3 = S_2^T + X_3$ is then found by convoluting the distributions of S_2^T and X_3, and the process continues.

Note that after the first step the total probability assigned to the values of S_k is not necessarily equal to one. Instead, the total should equal C_{k-1}, the probability of continuing beyond step k−1.

The cycle terminates when either a prespecified truncation value is reached or when C_k is so small that, for practical purposes, we are assured that a point has been reached when the process will have stopped. Upon termination, several values of interest may be calculated, such as

$$P\{\text{Reject } H_0\} = \sum R_k = 1 - P\{\text{Accept } H_0\}$$
$$\text{ASN} = E\{N\} = \sum k P\{\text{Test stops at step k}\} = \sum k(R_k + A_k)$$
$$\text{Var}(N) = \sum k^2(R_k + A_k) - (\text{ASN})^2.$$

Example 5.1:

Suppose that attributes sampling is conducted to test H_0: $p = 0.1$ versus H_1: $p = 0.5$ where p represents the proportion of nonconforming items in a large lot. Allowable producer's and consumer's risks are specified as $\alpha = \beta \approx 0.20$. Let X_i equal 0 if the ith item inspected is conforming, 1 if nonconforming. Using equations (4-4), appropriate linear boundaries for rejection and acceptance are given by

$$L_n = -0.6309 + 0.2675n$$
$$U_n = 0.6309 + 0.2675n.$$

Table 5: Exact OC and ASN Calculations Using the Direct Method

	x_k	$P\{X_k=x_k\}$	s_k	$P\{S_k=s_k\}$	R_k	A_k	C_k	s_k^T	$P\{S_k^T=s_k^T\}$
k=1	0	.9	0	.9	.1	.0	.9	0	.9
	1	.1	1*	.1					
k=2	0	.9	0	.81	.0	.0	.9	0	.81
	1	.1	1	.09				1	.09
k=3	0	.9	0**	.729	.009	.729	.162	1	.162
	1	.1	1	.165					
			2*	.009					
k=4	0	.9	1	.1458	.0162	.0	.1458	1	.1458
	1	.1	2*	.0162					
k=5	0	.9	1	.13122	.01458	.0	.13122	1	.13122
	1	.1	2*	.01458					
k=6	0	.9	1**	.118096	.013122	.118096	.0	**Process Stops**	
	1	.1	2*	.013122		_____			

$$P\{Accept\ H_0\} = \ \ .847$$

$$ASN = 1(.1) + 2(0) + 3(.738) + 4(.0162) + 5(.01458) + 6(.131218) = 3.24$$

$$Variance = 1^2(.1) + 2^2(0) + 3^2(.738) + 4^2(.0162) + 5^2(.01458) + 6^2(.131218) - (3.24)^2 = 1.59$$

---

*A result where (k,S_k) falls in the "stop and reject" region.

**A result where (k,S_k) falls in the "stop and accept" region.

Figure 21: Sequential Plan, Direct Method Example

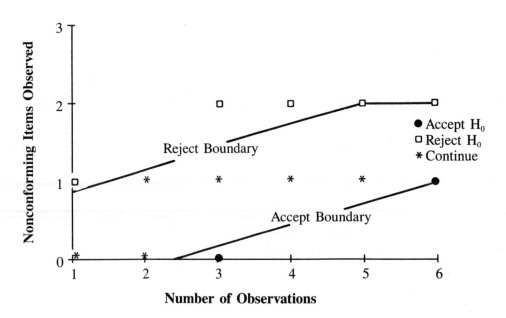

Suppose that these boundaries are used and that the process is truncated at the 6th observation. This plan is presented graphically in Figure 21. Table 5 illustrates the calculation of OC and ASN values when, for example, H_0 is true and p is equal to 0.10. Resulting values are P{Accept H_0} = 0.847 and ASN = 3.24 at p = 0.10. When H_1 is true and p equals 0.50, similar calculations yield P{Accept H_0} = 0.156 and ASN = 2.44. These calculations can be repeated, at other p values of interest, to generate the complete OC and ASN functions.

The truncated plan is quite conservative with respect to the specified risk probabilities, yielding actual α and β values of 0.153 and 0.156. If a plan is desired with actual risk probabilities closer to the specified values of $\alpha = \beta = 0.20$, the boundaries of Wald's plan can be modified in any way and the direct method can be used to recalculate α and β for the revised plan.

For the example presented above, which is based on attributes sampling (sampling from a discrete distribution), the direct method calculations are straightforward. A FORTRAN program which calculates OC and ASN values, assuming that linear boundaries are used for the sequential test, can be found in Appendix B. As the distribution of the X_i becomes more complex, so do the necessary calculations. The Poisson distribution is somewhat more difficult since, although it is also a discrete distribution, each X_i has an infinite number of possible values. Continuous distributions present further problems, as the convolution process requires numerical integration. A survey of direct method applications can be found in Aroian (1976).

6. Sequential Estimation

Basic statistical applications tend to fall into two broad categories: hypothesis testing and estimation. The primary focus of this text is on hypothesis testing, with little attention paid to estimation. There are two reasons for this approach:

(1) The primary advantage of the sequential approach is the ability, in a hypothesis testing application, to make a decision based on fewer observations than a fixed sample size test would require *without degrading the test's OC function.* A similar advantage *does not exist* in the case of sequential-based estimation. Suppose that in Example 4.1 the sequential test terminates after 50 observations with an "accept the lot" decision (recall that a comparable fixed sample size plan would require 80 observations). The sequential test's decision, based on the 50 observations, is as likely to be correct as a decision based on the 80-observation fixed sample size test. However, an *estimate* of the true proportion of nonconforming items p based on the same 50 observations will *not* have the accuracy of an estimate based on 80 observations. At best, the sequential-based estimate would have the accuracy of a 50-observation fixed sample size estimate.

(2) Calculations can be quite complex and are beyond the scope of this text. Simple, intuitive estimators ($\overline{X}$ for μ, s for σ, etc.) that have desirable statistical properties (such as unbiasedness or minimum variance) in the case of fixed sample size estimation generally lose these properties if their calculation is based on observations from a sequential hypothesis test. The usual formulas for point estimates and confidence intervals are no longer appropriate. In addition, some sequential-based estimation procedures require a *Bayesian* approach, which is not dealt with in this text.

Sequential estimation problems fall into two categories. In the situation of item (1), the estimate is a *by-product* of a sequential hypothesis test. The primary concern is the "accept" or "reject" decision. A second category is sequential estimation *for its own sake,* with no related hypothesis test.

Aroian's (1976) survey paper on direct method applications gives several references which involve the use of the direct method to estimate parameters following sequential tests. Siegmund (1978) gives formulas for approximately unbiased estimators of a process mean following a two-sided hypothesis test. Schmee (1980) shows how to estimate the mean time between failures following the sequential life-testing plans of MIL-STD-781C. The following approach is an example of estimation for its own sake, where an estimate of a process mean is required.

Fixed-Width Estimation of a Process Mean

Suppose that a confidence interval estimate of a process mean μ having specified total width 2d is required (the interval will have the form $\overline{X} \pm d$). Siegmund (1985) presents an estimation procedure which assumes that the process standard deviation σ is unknown. To find an approximate $100(1-\alpha)$ percent confidence interval of width 2d, calculate

$$a_0 = 2.68 + 0.5\, z_{\alpha/2}^2 \qquad\qquad a_k = 1 - \frac{a_0}{k} \qquad\qquad k = 1, 2, \ldots \qquad (6\text{-}1)$$

The "stopping rule" which determines when to terminate the sampling process is based on the statistic

$$S_k = \sum_{i=1}^{k} (X_i - \overline{X}_k)^2 \qquad\qquad (6\text{-}2)$$

where $\overline{X}_k$ is the sample mean of the first k observations. Sampling continues until $S_k \leq b_k$ where

$$b_k = a_k\, d^2 k^2 / z_{\alpha/2}^2. \qquad\qquad (6\text{-}3)$$

Let N represent the observation number at which this condition is met. The approximate $100(1-\alpha)$ percent confidence interval is given by $\overline{X}_N \pm d$. The ASN is approximately equal to $(n_0 + a_0 - 2.2)$ where $n_0 = (z_{\alpha/2}\sigma/d)^2$. This is the formula from basic statistics for the required sample size to estimate μ with confidence interval width 2d in the case where σ is known. The sequential procedure, which assumes an unknown σ, results in roughly the same number of required observations. A minimum of four observations are required for the sequential estimation procedure to be valid.

Example 6.1:

Suppose we wish to estimate the process mean μ with a 95 percent confidence interval of total width $2d = 1.0$. Then $z_{\alpha/2} = 1.96$ and $a_0 = 2.68 + 0.5(1.96)^2 = 4.601$. Table 6 shows the appropriate values of $\{a_k\}$ and stopping boundaries $\{b_k\}$, along with example results. The process terminates after the 68th observation. The approximate 95 percent confidence interval for the mean is then given by

$$20.27 \pm 0.50 = (19.77, 20.77).$$

Table 6: Sequential Fixed-Width Estimation: Boundaries and Sample Results

$$z_{\alpha/2} = 1.96 \qquad d = 0.5$$

Observation (k)	a_k	X_k	$\overline{X}_k$	$b_k{}^*$	S_k	
1	-3.60	18.43	18.43		0.0	
2	-1.30	18.44	18.44		0.0	
3	-0.53	19.84	18.90		1.3	
4	-0.15	22.22	19.73	-0.2	9.6	
5	0.08	19.18	19.62	0.1	9.8	
6	0.23	22.57	20.11	0.5	17.1	
7	0.34	24.36	20.72	1.1	32.5	
8	0.43	21.37	20.80	1.8	32.9	
9	0.49	16.64	20.34	2.6	48.3	
10	0.54	20.66	20.37	3.5	48.4	
11	0.58	16.88	20.05	4.6	59.4	
•	•	•	•	•	•	
•	•	•	•	•	•	
•	•	•	•	•	•	
63	0.93	19.77	20.32	239.4	259.8	
64	0.93	17.07	20.27	247.4	270.2	
65	0.93	19.21	20.26	255.5	271.4	
66	0.93	19.08	20.24	263.7	272.7	
67	0.93	20.02	20.24	272.1	272.8	
68	0.93	22.72	20.27	280.6	278.8	***Terminate Process!

*Terminate the process as soon as $S_k \leq b_k$.

A brief simulation study was also performed to evaluate the performance of this approximate estimation procedure. The study assumed that σ was equal to 2.0, so a fixed sample size procedure would require $n_0 = [(1.96)(2.0)/0.5]^2 = 61.5$ or 62 observations. The expected ASN for the sequential procedure is given by ASN = $(61.5 + 4.6 - 2.2) = 63.9$ observations. The study, based on 2,000 simulated confidence intervals, was quite consistent with these expectations with an empirical ASN of 64.1 and a confidence value of 94.5 percent.

7. References

Alexander, R., and R. Suich. "A Truncated Sequential t-Test for General α and β." *Technometrics* 15 (1973): 79-86. (Treats the general case where $\alpha \neq \beta$ and includes two-sided test procedures.)

Armitage, P. "Restricted Sequential Procedures." *Biometrika* 44 (1957): 9-26. (Truncated procedures for testing a process mean and for comparing two proportions.)

Armitage, P. *Sequential Medical Trials,* 2nd ed. New York: John Wiley & Sons, 1975. (Extensive treatment of sequential testing and estimation with applications to medical experiments.)

Aroian, L.A. "Sequential Analysis, Direct Method." *Technometrics* 10 (1968): 125-132. (Presentation of the direct method with applications to sampling from the normal and binomial distributions.)

Aroian, L.A. "Applications of the Direct Method in Sequential Analysis." *Technometrics* 18 (1976): 301-306. (Comprehensive survey of direct method applications with an extensive bibliography.)

Aroian, L.A., and D. Oksoy. *Exact Sequential Methods for the Comparison of Two Medical Treatments.* Schenectady, New York: Administrative and Engineering Systems Monograph AES-7504, Union College and University, 1975. (An alternative to Armitage's test for comparing proportions.)

Aroian, L.A., and D.E. Robison. "Direct Methods for Exact Truncated Sequential Tests of the Mean of a Normal Distribution." *Technometrics* 11 (1969): 661-675. (Includes tables for test plan parameters along with OC and ASN values.)

Burr, I.W. *Statistical Quality Control Methods.* New York: Marcel Dekker, 1976. (Contains a sequential analysis chapter emphasizing Wald-style plans and approximation formulas for OC and ASN values.)

Epstein, B. *Statistical Techniques in Life Testing.* Detroit: Wayne State University, Technical Report No. 3, Office of Naval Research, Department of Mathematics, 1958. (Includes material regarding truncation values and operating characteristic curves of sequential life tests.)

Epstein, B., and M. Sobel. "Sequential Life Tests in the Exponential Case." *Annals of Mathematical Statistics* 26 (1955): 82-93. (Life testing based on sampling with and without replacement, including several examples.)

Garrison, D.R., and J.J. Hickey. "Wald Sequential Sampling for Attribute Inspection." *Journal of Quality Technology* 16 (1984): 172-174. (BASIC computer program to generate sequential plans and approximate OC and ASN values for binomial sampling.)

Goss, T.I. *Truncated Sequential Test for the Variance of a Normal Distribution with Applications to Maintainability.* Schenectady, New York: Administrative and Engineering Systems Monograph AES-746, Union College and University, Schenectady, 1973. (Includes tables of truncated test plans and their OC and ASN values, along with a FORTRAN program to generate plans.)

Grant, E.L., and R.S. Leavenworth. *Statistical Quality Control.* New York: McGraw-Hill Book Co., 1980. (Brief treatment of sequential plans for attribute sampling and life testing.)

Hearron, A.E., G.L. Elfring, and J.R. Schultz. "Biopharmaceutical Applications of Group Sequential Designs." *Communications in Statistics: Theory and Methods* 13 No. 9 (1984): 2419-2450. (Plans for testing a proportion, comparing proportions, and comparing means applied to medical trials.)

Meeker, W.Q. *Sequential Tests of the Hypergeometric Distribution.* Schenectady, New York: Administrative and Engineering Systems Monograph AES-7506, Union College and University, 1975. (A comprehensive treatment with supporting FORTRAN programs.)

MIL-STD-105D (1963). *Sampling Procedures and Tables for Inspection by Attributes.* U.S. Government Printing Office: 1980-603-121/4090. (Widely used reference for single, double, and multiple sampling plans.)

MIL-STD-781C (1977). *Reliability Design Qualification and Production Acceptance Tests: Exponential Distribution.* U.S. Department of Defense, AMSC #22333. (Ordinary and sequential life testing plans.)

Schmee, J. "MIL-STD-781 and Confidence Intervals." *Journal of Quality Technology* 12 (1980): 98-105. (Estimation of mean lifetime following sequential life testing.)

Siegmund, D. "Estimation Following Sequential Tests." *Biometrika* 65 (1978): 341-349. (Estimation of a normal mean following Armitage's sequential test.)

Siegmund, D. *Sequential Analysis: Tests and Confidence Intervals,* New York: Springer-Verlag, 1985. (Modern, technical treatment of sequential methods. Includes generalizations of Wald procedures and a detailed treatment of sequential estimation.)

Suich, R., and B. Iglewicz. "A Truncated Sequential t-Test." *Technometrics* 12 (1970): 789-798. (Includes one- and two-sided procedures.)

Wald, A. *Sequential Analysis.* New York: John Wiley & Sons, 1947. (Classic introduction to sequential procedures.)

Wetherill, G.B., and K.D. Glazebrook. *Sequential Methods in Statistics.* New York: Chapman and Hall, 1986. (Comprehensive, modern treatment of sequential testing and estimation. Includes many example applications.)

Woodall, R.C., and B.M. Kurkjian. "Exact Operating Characteristic for Truncated Sequential Life Tests in the Exponential Case." *Annals of Mathematical Statistics* 33 (1962): 1403-1412. (Assumes that testing is conducted with replacement; includes a numerical example.)

Appendix A: OC and ASN Function Approximation Formulas

The formulas given in this Appendix are all based on a general approximation procedure originally developed by Wald (1947). The procedure makes the assumption that, when termination occurs in a sequential test plan, the test statistic is *exactly* equal to either the accept or reject boundary. The assumption was necessary to obtain workable approximation formulas, but is not correct and will in many cases lead to approximations that are not particularly accurate. If anything beyond crude approximations of OC and ASN values is required, the more recent direct method or computer simulation techniques should be used.

Binomial Sampling

The OC curve can be approximated at any value of p by calculating

$$P_A(p) = (A^{h(p)} - 1)/(A^{h(p)} - B^{h(p)}) \tag{A-1}$$

where h(p) is a function of p which satisfies the relation

$$p = \frac{1 - \left(\frac{1 - p_1}{1 - p_0}\right)^{h(p)}}{\left(\frac{p_1}{p_0}\right)^{h(p)} - \left(\frac{1 - p_1}{1 - p_0}\right)^{h(p)}}. \tag{A-2}$$

Once $P_A(p)$ has been found, ASN values are calculated according to

$$ASN(p) = \{a(1 - P_A(p)) - bP_A(p)\}/\{pr_1 - (1 - p)r_2\}. \tag{A-3}$$

Recall that $A = (1 - \beta)/\alpha$ and $B = \beta/(1 - \alpha)$. Terms a, b, r_1, and r_2 are defined in equations (4-4).

Although h(p) can be found numerically for any specified p-value of interest, it is easier to specify a value of h(p), use (A-2) to calculate the corresponding value of p, and then calculate the approximate acceptance probability and OC value. Specific h(p) values were used to obtain the five-point approximation formulas of Section 4.1.1: when h(p) = +1.0, p = p_0; when h(p) = −1.0, p = p_1; and when h(p) → 0, p → s. To calculate another point on the OC curve, let h(p) = 0.5. Then (A-2) is used to obtain p = 0.016 and (A-1) is evaluated at h(p) = 0.5 to obtain an approximate acceptance probability, when p = 0.016, of $P_A(p)$ = 0.86. This compares to an exact result, using the direct method, of 0.8987. Substituting 0.86 into (A-3) gives an approximate ASN value of 89.40. This compares to an exact result, using the direct method, of 99.71 (the approximation formula underestimates the exact value by 10 percent). This process can be repeated to obtain entire approximate OC and ASN functions.

Poisson Sampling

The OC curve can be approximated at any value of λ by calculating

$$P_A(\lambda) = (A^{h(\lambda)} - 1)/(A^{h(\lambda)} - B^{h(\lambda)}) \tag{A-4}$$

where h(λ) is a function of λ which satisfies the equation

$$\lambda = \{h(\lambda)(\lambda_1 - \lambda_0)\}/\{(\lambda_1/\lambda_0)^{h(\lambda)} - 1\}. \tag{A-5}$$

Once $P_A(\lambda)$ has been calculated, ASN values are found according to

$$ASN(\lambda) = \{a(1 - P_A(\lambda)) - bP_A(\lambda)\}/\{\lambda_0 - \lambda_1 + \lambda r\}. \tag{A-6}$$

Once again, $A = (1 - \beta)/\alpha$ and $B = \beta/(1 - \alpha)$. Terms a, b, and r are defined in equations (4-12).

As in the binomial case, the easiest approach is to first specify a value for h(λ), calculate the corresponding value of λ, and then calculate the approximate acceptance probability. Specifying h(λ) equal to +1.0, 0.0, and −1.0 leads to the five-point approximation formulas at λ_0, s, and λ_1, respectively. To calculate another point on the OC curve, let h(λ) = 0.5. Then (A-5) is evaluated to obtain $\lambda = 1.21$ and (A-4) is evaluated at $h(\lambda) = 0.5$ to obtain an approximate acceptance probability, when $\lambda = 1.21$, of 0.84. The exact probability, using the direct method, is 0.8747. Substituting 0.84 into (A-6) results in an approximate ASN value of 8.89. This compares to an exact result, using the direct method, of 11.59. This process can be repeated to generate entire approximate OC or ASN functions.

Normal, Testing for Process Mean, σ Known

The OC and ASN functions can be approximated at any value of μ. For the OC function, calculate

$$P_A(\mu) = (A^{h(\mu)} - 1)/(A^{h(\mu)} - B^{h(\mu)}) \tag{A-7}$$

where

$$h(\mu) = \{-2\mu(\mu_1 - \mu_0) + \mu_1{}^2 - \mu_0{}^2\}/(\mu_1 - \mu_0)^2. \tag{A-8}$$

The ASN function is given by

$$ASN(\mu) = -2\sigma^2\{a(1 - P_A(\mu)) - bP_A(\mu)\}/\{h(\mu)(\mu_1 - \mu_0)^2\} \tag{A-9}$$

where $A = (1 - \beta)/\alpha$, $B = \beta/(1 - \alpha)$, and terms a and b are defined in equations (4-16).

As an example, consider the value $\mu = 20.1$ and calculate $h(\mu) = 0.600$ from equation (A-8). Substituting 0.600 into (A-7) gives an approximate value for $P_A(\mu)$ of 0.86, compared to a fixed sample size test acceptance probability, at the same μ value, of 0.854. Equation (A-9) gives an approximate ASN of 20.6. This process can be repeated to generate an entire approximate OC function.

Normal, Testing for Process Variability, σ Known

The OC and ASN functions can be approximated at *any* value of σ. For the OC function, calculate

$$P_A(\sigma) = (A^{h(\sigma)} - 1)/(A^{h(\sigma)} - B^{h(\sigma)}) \tag{A-10}$$

where $h(\sigma)$ is the solution to the equation

$$\sigma^2 = [1 - (\sigma_0{}^2/\sigma_1{}^2)^{h(\sigma)}]/[h(\sigma)(1/\sigma_0{}^2 - 1/\sigma_1{}^2)]. \tag{A-11}$$

The ASN function is given by

$$ASN(\sigma) = \{a(1 - P_A(\sigma)) - bP_A(\sigma)\}/\{\ln(\sigma_0/\sigma_1) + \sigma^2(1/\sigma_0{}^2 - 1/\sigma_1{}^2)/2\}. \tag{A-12}$$

where $A = (1 - \beta)/\alpha$, $B = \beta/(1 - \alpha,)$ and terms a and b are defined in equations (4-20). The easiest approach is to specify a value for $h(\sigma)$, calculate the corresponding value of σ according to (A-11), and then proceed. Note that when $h(\sigma) = +1.0$, $\sigma = \sigma_0$; when $h(\sigma) = -1.0$, $\sigma = \sigma_1$; and when $h(\sigma) = 0.0$, $\sigma = \sqrt{s}$. These values were used to arrive at the five-point approximation formulas. As another example, when $h(\sigma) = 0.8$, equation (A-11) yields $\sigma = 0.104$ and we calculate, using (A-10), an approximate value for $P_A(\sigma)$ of 0.85. This compares to a fixed sample size test acceptance probability, at the same σ value, of 0.83. Equation (A-12) gives an approximate ASN of 19.7, compared to the fixed sample size value of 28. This process can be repeated to generate an entire approximate OC or ASN function.

Life Testing

The OC and ATT functions can be approximated at *any* value of θ. For the OC function, calculate

$$P_A(\theta) = (A^{h(\theta)} - 1)/(A^{h(\theta)} - B^{h(\theta)}) \tag{A-13}$$

where $h(\theta)$ is the solution to the equation

$$\theta = \{(\theta_0/\theta_1)^{h(\theta)} - 1\}/\{h(\theta)(1/\theta_1 - 1/\theta_0)\} \tag{A-14}$$

and $A = (1 - \beta)/\alpha$, $B = \beta/(1 - \alpha)$.

The easiest approach is to select a value for h(θ) and then determine the corresponding θ and acceptance probability. For example, if h(θ) = 0.6, then (A-14) gives θ = 5832 and (A-13) yields an approximate $P_A(\theta)$ value of 0.854. Once the acceptance probability has been determined, the approximate ATT can be calculated according to

$$ATT(\theta) = \theta\{h_2 - P_A(\theta)(h_1 + h_2)\}/(s - \theta) \qquad s \neq \theta \qquad (A\text{-}15)$$

where h_1, h_2, and s are defined in equations (4-23). Continuing the example where θ = 5832, calculate ATT(θ) $\approx$ 26631.

Appendix B: A Program to Calculate OC and ASN Functions for the Binomial Sampling Model

This program uses the direct method to evaluate OC and ASN functions for sequential tests of

$$H_0: p = p_0 \text{ versus } H_1: p = p_1$$

where $p_0 < p_1$. The user must supply the range of values for p for which the function is to be calculated and the increment between values (PLOW, PHIGH, and PDEL). The probability that the random sample size (the DSN) exceeds any specified value M can be calculated if required. Subroutine BOUNDS is used to calculate, given any observation number I, the boundaries of the sequential test plan.

Two versions of BOUNDS are provided. The first assumes that Wald-style parallel line boundaries are used, with the option of truncating (truncated plans are curtailed when the reject decision becomes inevitable, as illustrated in Figure 5). The second is designed to illustrate the versatility of the direct method, applying it to double sampling plans. Fixed sample size plans can also be evaluated using this subroutine and appropriate input parameters, as illustrated in Example B-3. In fact, any sequential test plan can be used by rewriting BOUNDS with no changes to the main program.

Program Listing

```
C   PROGRAM TO EVALUATE OC CURVES, USING THE DIRECT METHOD, FOR ONE-
C     SIDED SEQUENTIAL HYPOTHESIS TESTS BASED ON BINOMIAL SAMPLING.
C     (H0:  P = P0; H1: P = P1  WHERE P1 > P0).  REQUIRES INPUT OF
C     RANGE OF P-VALUES OF INTEREST AND, AS CURRENTLY PROGRAMMED,
C     BOUNDARIES OF WALD LINES.  TRUNCATION IS ALLOWED.  OTHER
C     TYPES OF BOUNDARIES CAN BE USED BY REPROGRAMMING SUBROUTINE
C     "BOUNDS".
      DIMENSION POLD(250),PNEW(250)
      INTEGER ULIM,BLOW,BHIGH,BHIGH1,BLOW1
    5 CONTINUE
      NEW = 1
      NEW1=1
      WRITE(5,2070)
 2070 FORMAT(/,' INPUT PLOW, PHIGH, AND PDEL')
      READ(5,*)PLOW,PHIGH,PDEL
      WRITE(5,2060)
 2060 FORMAT(/,' IF YOU WISH P(N>M), INPUT M.  ELSE INPUT ZERO.')
      READ(5,*)MCONT
        GVAL = 0.0
        IF(MCONT.EQ.0)GVAL = 1.0
      PR = PLOW - PDEL
   10 CONTINUE
      PR = PR + PDEL
      IF(PR.GT.(PHIGH+.5*PDEL))STOP
      J1=0
      J2=1
      NRNG=2
      PNEW(1) = 1. - PR
      PNEW(2) = PR
      ACC = 0.0
      REJ = 0.0
      ASN = 0.0
      VAR = 0.0
      DO 1000 I = 1,2000
        IVAL = I
        CALL BOUNDS(NEW,IVAL,BLOW,BHIGH)
        NEW = 0
        PJ2 = 0.0
        IF(J2.LE.BHIGH)GOTO 100
        BHIGH1 = BHIGH + 1
        DO 50 J = BHIGH1,J2
   50     PJ2 = PJ2 + PNEW(J-J1+1)
        REJ = REJ + PJ2
        J2 = BHIGH
```

```
      100    CONTINUE
             NLOW = 0
             PJ1 = 0.0
             IF(J1.GE.BLOW)GOTO 200
             NLOW = BLOW - J1
             BLOW1 = BLOW - 1
             DO 150 J = J1,BLOW1
      150       PJ1 = PJ1 + PNEW(J-J1+1)
             ACC = ACC + PJ1
             J1 = BLOW
      200    CONTINUE
             ASN = ASN + FLOAT(I)*(PJ1+PJ2)
               VAR = FLOAT(I*I)*(PJ1+PJ2) + VAR
             NRNG = J2 - J1 + 1
          IF(NRNG.GT.250)WRITE(5,2001)
     2001 FORMAT(' INTERNAL RANGE CAPACITY OF 250 EXCEEDED',/)
             CONT = 0.0
             DO 250 J = 1,NRNG
      250       CONT = CONT + PNEW(NLOW+J)
          IF(I.EQ.MCONT)GVAL=CONT
               IF(CONT.LT..0001)GOTO 700
          IF(NRNG.LE.0)GOTO 700
             DO 300 J =1,NRNG
                POLD(J) = PNEW(NLOW+J)
      300       CONTINUE
             NRNG = NRNG + 1
             J2 = J2 + 1
             PNEW(1) = POLD(1)*(1.-PR)
             PNEW(NRNG) = POLD(NRNG-1)*PR
          IF(NRNG.LE.2)GOTO 450
             DO 400 J = 2,NRNG-1
      400       PNEW(J) = POLD(J)*(1.-PR) + POLD(J-1)*PR
      450 CONTINUE
     1000 CONTINUE
      700 CONTINUE
             VAR = VAR - ASN*ASN
               IF(VAR.LT.0.0)VAR = 0.0
             STD = SQRT(VAR)
             IF(NEW1.EQ.1)WRITE(5,889)MCONT
      889 FORMAT(//,4X,'P',5X,' ACC. PR.',3X,'REJ. PR.',6X,
         1'ASN',5X,'S.D.',4X,'P(N > ',I3,')',/)
             NEW1=0
             WRITE(5,2090)PR,ACC,REJ,ASN,STD,GVAL
     2090 FORMAT(1X,F6.3,4X,F6.4,6X,F6.4,4X,F6.2,4X,
         *F5.2,6X,F6.4)
             GOTO 10
             END
```

Subroutine Bounds, Wald Boundaries

```
          SUBROUTINE BOUNDS(NEW,I,IBL,IBH)
C    ************************************************************
C    SUBROUTINE TO PROVIDE BOUNDARIES FOR SEQUENTIAL DECISION RULE.
C      REQUESTS SLOPE AND TWO INTERCEPTS FOR WALD RULE.
C      RETURNS LOWER BOUNDARY (ACCEPT LINE) AND UPPER BOUNDARY
C      (REJECT LINE) WHEN GIVEN I (SAMPLE NUMBER).
C      TEST SHOULD REJECT IF # OF DEFECTS OBSERVED IS STRICTLY GREATER
C      THAN UPPER BOUNDARY IBH (AN INTEGER VALUE); ACCEPT IF # OF
C      DEFECTS IS STRICTLY LESS THAN LOWER BOUNDARY IBL (INTEGER).
C    ************************************************************
  100 IF(NEW.EQ.0)GOTO 150
C
C    INPUT WALD PARAMETERS, TRUNCATION INFO ON FIRST CALL TO BOUNDS
C
```

```
          WRITE(5,2000)
 2000 FORMAT(/,' INPUT COMMON SLOPE, ACCEPT INTERCEPT, REJ. INTER.')
          READ(5,*)SL,AINT,RINT
          WRITE(5,2001)
 2001 FORMAT(/,' INPUT TRUNCATION VALUE AND REJECT NUMBER',/,
     1'    (-1 IF DECISION BASED ON CLOSEST BOUNDARY)')
          READ(5,*)MVAL,IREJ
          IF(IREJ.NE.-1)GOTO 150
            AVG = (AINT + RINT)/2. + SL*FLOAT(MVAL)
            IREJ = AVG + 1
   150 CONTINUE
C
C    CALCULATE LINEAR WALD BOUNDARIES
C
          VA = FLOAT(I)*SL
          VLOW = VA + AINT
          IF(VLOW.LT.0.0)GOTO 205
            IBL = VLOW+1.
          GOTO 210
   205    IBL = 0
   210 CONTINUE
          VHIGH = VA + RINT
          IBH = VHIGH
          IF(IBH.GT.(IREJ-1))IBH = IREJ-1
C
C    CHECK FOR TRUNCATION POINT
C
          IF(I.NE.MVAL)RETURN
C
C    TRUNCATE ACCORDING TO USER-SUPPLIED REJECTION CRITERIA
C
   200    IBL = IREJ
            IBH = IREJ - 1
          RETURN
          END
```

Subroutine Bounds, Double Sampling

```
          SUBROUTINE BOUNDS(NEW,I,IBL,IBH)
C    *********************************************************************
C    SUBROUTINE TO PROVIDE BOUNDARIES FOR SEQUENTIAL DECISION RULE.
C     REQUESTS PARAMETERS FOR DOUBLE SAMPLING PLAN.
C     RETURNS LOWER BOUNDARY (ACCEPT VALUE) AND UPPER BOUNDARY
C     (REJECT VALUE) WHEN GIVEN I (SAMPLE NUMBER).
C     TEST SHOULD REJECT IF # OF DEFECTS OBSERVED IS STRICTLY GREATER
C     THAN UPPER BOUNDARY IBH (AN INTEGER VALUE); ACCEPT IF # OF
C     DEFECTS IS STRICTLY LESS THAN LOWER BOUNDARY IBL (INTEGER).
C    *********************************************************************
   100 IF(NEW.EQ.0)GOTO 150
C
C    INPUT PARAMETERS FOR DOUBLE SAMPLING PLAN
C
          WRITE(5,2000)
 2000 FORMAT(/,' INPUT 1ST SS, REJ #, ACC #, 2ND SS, REJ #')
          READ(5,*)N1,IR1,IA1,N2,IR2
   150 CONTINUE
C
C    CALCULATE BOUNDARIES
```

```
C
      IF(I.EQ.N1)GOTO 205
      IF(I.EQ.(N1+N2))GOTO 210
        IBL = 0
        IBH = 999999
        RETURN
  205   IBL = IA1 + 1
        IBH = IR1 - 1
        RETURN
  210   IBL = IR2
        IBH = IR2 - 1
      RETURN
      END
```

Example B-1:

This example uses the parallel boundaries of Example 4.1, with truncation according to the fixed
sample size plan (n = 80) of Example 2.1. By specifying M = 79, the probability of reaching
the truncation value of 80 is also calculated for each value of p.

```
$ RUN SHORT

INPUT PLOW, PHIGH, AND PDEL
.01 .08 .01

IF YOU WISH P(N>M), INPUT M.  ELSE INPUT ZERO.
79

INPUT COMMON SLOPE, ACCEPT INTERCEPT, REJ. INTER.
.028  -1.06  1.58

INPUT TRUNCATION VALUE AND REJECT NUMBER
  (-1 IF DECISION BASED ON CLOSEST BOUNDARY)
80 3
```

P	ACC. PR.	REJ. PR.	ASN	S.D.	P(N > 79)
0.010	0.9554	0.0446	48.86	17.54	0.0913
0.020	0.8018	0.1982	53.26	20.01	0.1672
0.030	0.6033	0.3967	52.68	21.23	0.1707
0.040	0.4204	0.5796	49.31	22.09	0.1367
0.050	0.2779	0.7221	44.79	22.36	0.0954
0.060	0.1773	0.8227	40.06	22.00	0.0608
0.070	0.1105	0.8895	35.61	21.15	0.0363
0.080	0.0680	0.9320	31.64	20.01	0.0206

Example B-2:

This example uses the double sampling plan of Example 2.3 (the second version of subroutine
BOUNDS is used). The choice of M = 99 (or any other value between n_1 and $n_1 + n_2$) allows
calculation of the probability that the second sample is required for each value of p.

```
$ RUN SHORT

INPUT PLOW, PHIGH, AND PDEL
.01 .08 .01

IF YOU WISH P(N>M), INPUT M.  ELSE INPUT ZERO.
99

INPUT 1ST SS, REJ #, ACC #, 2ND SS, REJ #
50 3 0 50 4
```

P	ACC. PR.	REJ. PR.	ASN	S.D.	P(N > 99)
0.010	0.9752	0.0248	69.06	24.28	0.3812
0.020	0.8433	0.1567	77.87	24.83	0.5574
0.030	0.6334	0.3666	79.64	24.57	0.5927
0.040	0.4236	0.5764	77.34	24.89	0.5468
0.050	0.2594	0.7406	73.18	24.93	0.4636
0.060	0.1485	0.8515	68.55	24.15	0.3709
0.070	0.0809	0.9191	64.21	22.55	0.2842
0.080	0.0425	0.9575	60.53	20.38	0.2105

Example B-3:

In this example, the double sampling plan subroutine is used to evaluate the fixed sample size plan of Example 2.1. Since the first sample has an accept number of 2 and a reject number of 3, the decision will always be made based on this sample and the second sample will never be required. To satisfy the program's input variable requirements, arbitrary positive integers should be used for the second sample's size and reject number.

```
$ RUN SHORT

INPUT PLOW, PHIGH, AND PDEL
.01 .08 .01

IF YOU WISH P(N>M), INPUT M.  ELSE INPUT ZERO.
0

INPUT 1ST SS, REJ #, ACC #, 2ND SS, REJ #
80 3 2 99 5
```

P	ACC. PR.	REJ. PR.	ASN	S.D.	P(N > 0)
0.010	0.9534	0.0466	80.00	0.00	1.0000
0.020	0.7844	0.2156	80.00	0.00	1.0000
0.030	0.5681	0.4319	80.00	0.00	1.0000
0.040	0.3748	0.6252	80.00	0.10	1.0000
0.050	0.2306	0.7694	80.00	0.06	1.0000
0.060	0.1344	0.8656	80.00	0.00	1.0000
0.070	0.0750	0.9250	80.00	0.00	1.0000
0.080	0.0404	0.9596	80.00	0.00	1.0000

Index